THE
UGLY
GAME

THE
UGLY
GAME

How football lost its magic
and what it could learn
from the NFL

MARTIN CALLADINE

First published by Pitch Publishing, 2015

Pitch Publishing
A2 Yeoman Gate
Yeoman Way
Durrington
BN13 3QZ
www.pitchpublishing.co.uk

A CIP catalogue record is available for this book
from the British Library.

ISBN 978 178531-007-2

Typesetting and origination by Pitch Publishing

Printed in Great Britain

To my dad, who hated all sport and would've had no interest whatsoever in the contents of this book, but would nonetheless have been very proud to see it published.

John Calladine (1948–2014)

Contents

Introduction

A FEW years ago I fell out of love not just with my football team, but with football altogether. With going to games, with *Match of the Day*, with 5 Live and midweek Champions League games, with the Premier League and La Liga, with Messi and Ronaldo, with the transfer window, with third-round day and the Road to Wembley. All of it.

This season, after living apart from football for several years, I got a proper divorce. I no longer know the name of my team's reserve left-back. I've no idea who Crystal Palace's assistant manager is. I couldn't even tell you England's current centre midfield pairing, let alone who I think it should actually be.

You may not have gone that far yourself, but if you've been married to the game for a long time I bet you've had at least a few rough patches. And I imagine you can identify, at least in part, with why it happened to me, and why I came to see that football was no longer the Beautiful Game.

* * * * *

With the sound down, football is a strange, otherworldly experience, like a computer simulation patiently mapping all the ways 22 men can be arranged on a patch of grass. If you are sleep-deprived, the effect is particularly pronounced, with the ball appearing to ping about as if compelled not by the players but sinister external influences. Doubly so if Stoke are playing.

It was 3am and I was awake again. In just a few hours I would have to be up for work on Monday morning. I flipped around the channels, hoping for the original *Die Hard* or *Predator*; something exciting enough to keep me awake but so completely familiar that I could switch off mentally and get back to sleep immediately my daughter's night-time feed was finished.

I had Saturday's *Match of the Day* recorded, the epitome of mindless, predictable viewing. But after just a few minutes I switched it off, unable to care about how Manchester City or Chelsea or Aston Villa were doing (the last of these, I know, isn't necessarily an unusual state of mind). I didn't know if it was tiredness clouding my thoughts, but I felt like I could happily never watch a game of football again. My daughter was deep in her bottle, eyes almost closed, one tiny hand lightly stropping my t-shirt, gurgling like Andy Carroll after a night out. I clicked on Channel 4 at random and was greeted by something quite startling.

It was a slow-motion replay, so slow in fact that, at first, the screen appeared frozen. Rising from the back of the picture, illuminated by floodlights and camera flashes, a ball climbed into view, rotating on its axis with an almost mechanical intent and oblivious to the balletic violence of the rucking men below. As the ball traced a path towards the foreground, the camera began to pan, showing its trajectory, apex and eventual descent.

With impossible grace, an athlete appeared from below, so close to the camera he might almost have been in my lounge. He was already halfway through a smoothly executed leap, back arched like a high jumper, arms extended above his head, hands almost touching at the thumbs, fingers splayed. The ball made contact with his gloved fingertips, its spin deftly disarmed and the pass now ready to be pulled in.

At that moment, though, with the perfectly choreographed performance seemingly complete, another player appeared, little more than a blur in contrasting colours, and smashed into the catcher, shoulder first, with the force of a car t-boning another at a crossroads. The players ended in a heap, the ball rolled away and I winced in my seat, accidentally knocking the bottle's teat from my daughter's mouth so that the crowd's cheers and her protests became one.

The scene set off a series of rapid flashbacks that hit me like a Lee Cattermole tackle from behind. Memories of growing up in the 1980s. Memories of the NFL on Channel 4 presented by the wonderful Mick Luckhurst, a Brit abroad who, like a reverse Loyd Grossman, seemed permanently to be at war with his own speaking voice. Memories of getting to choose your own team, completely unconstrained by geography or family tradition. Memories of the Chicago Bears and The Fridge. Memories of rappers, whose records I wasn't allowed to play, wearing Raiders gear. Memories of pledging allegiance to Joe Montana or John Elway or Dan Marino. Memories of converting our daily lunchtime game of British Bulldogs into a rapidly-banned brawl with a ball. And, eventually, memories of starting going to my local league football club and putting all that shoulder-padded nonsense behind me.

I watched the rest of the game, my daughter asleep on my shoulder, and it felt like I'd been thrown a lifeline. I realised, with a warming sense of serenity, that I wasn't just overworked and dog-tired, but that I was completely sick of football. Bored with the England team, tired of hearing about Lampard and Gerrard's puzzling incompatibility, fed up with high ticket prices and atmosphereless games, angry at the financial ruin of so many once-great clubs, infuriated by the stockpiling of talent by a few title challengers and saddened by the total disregard for any notion of fairness.

So I returned to my childhood love: American football. I was amazed at what I discovered. Here was a game, the glitziest product of the most consumerist culture in the world, that, miraculously, seemed to be doing things the right way. At first it was difficult to acknowledge, like admitting to yourself that Robbie Savage has made a good point, but there was no avoiding it. The NFL is, I concluded, the closest thing to perfection there is in sport.

Football was the game of the 20th century, its elegant simplicity and universal appeal making it the first truly global sport. But, with the 21st century still young, it's a game showing its age, led astray by money; its self-interest making it increasingly a stranger to its audience.

The NFL, by contrast – despite its undeserved reputation among many as a silly pastime; a contrived vehicle for endless advertising – seems a sport able to handle money and fame without surrendering what sits at the heart of all great sports: a belief in open, fair competition.

In America you can buy almost anything. Anything that is but the Super Bowl. Because, remarkably, the NFL it is a sport where the worst team still gets the first pick of the best players. A sport where the amount clubs can spend is tightly controlled to prevent billionaires buying success. A sport where TV income is shared, where there's no prize money for winning the Super Bowl and where smaller clubs can hold on to their star players. A sport where young players have to earn their money, where black managers are the norm and where buying a team is more like a tightly regulated business than a used-car auction.

The NFL isn't without its flaws, of course. There's the legendary American distaste for draws[1], a lack of promotion or relegation, significant doping problems and a fixture system that can only be understood by those with a good pass at A Level maths.

But, like the growing army of British NFL fans – many of whom are also disenchanted with what the Premier League has become – I've found American football has rekindled my love of sport generally. It is, I'm going to argue in this book, a brilliant counter-example to those who feel that either nothing can be done about the direction of football or that any complaining is just pointless luddism.

To me, then, the NFL is a mirror into which English football must be forced to look. Not everything that happens there can or should be transposed to the Premier League; the solution to many of football's ills may be completely different. But there's no doubt in my mind that the NFL could be an invaluable provocation; a challenge to the people who run football to do better and to the fans who watch it to either fight harder for football's soul or be prepared to turn their backs on it.

This book assumes little knowledge of the NFL beyond a few basics, but a great deal of cumulative cultural exposure to football.[2] Each chapter examines football from a different aspect, contrasting it, often unfavourably, with what happens in the NFL. Sometimes the criticism is brutal, but it's mostly well-meant. I hope that it will be clear that I loved football (and still retain great affection for it), and that my anger and disappointment reflects the feeling that, rather than me leaving football, football left me.

One final note on terminology. When I refer to 'football', I always mean 'association football', never American football (despite my love of American sports, I'm not sure I could ever feel comfortable using the word 'soccer').

Welcome to *The Ugly Game*.

---

1   It's wonderful how upset draws make many American NFL fans. They happen no more than once or twice a year, yet are often greeted with perplexed and frustrated anger, like an Englishman being informed that a rail replacement service is in operation.

2   As I have found these last five years, following a near 20-year hiatus as a supporter, the NFL is an incredibly intricate sport, combining the best of rugby, basketball and Australian rules, with a level of tactical complexity that may exceed cricket.

1.

'I only expect one of you to come out of this room alive...'

Because a salary cap means you can't buy the title.

I USED to think that even Roman Abramovich despised John Terry. Despite his almost limitless riches, it must be galling – mustn't it? – to hand over more than £8m a year to a man whose very appearance seems to stir ancestral memories of the Victorian science of phrenology, with its belief that you might tell a criminal simply by the shape of his head.

And as soon as he's slid Terry a suitcase of undeserved riches over the table, there would've been another knock on the door. It's Frank Lampard's agent come to negotiate terms for another season of late bursts into the box and surprisingly accurate long-range shooting.

John Terry celebrating the collapse of the Soviet Union.

And will no one think of Sheikh Mansour? Not only is he paying Yaya Touré, Samir Nasri and Sergio Agüero more than the whole Swansea squad combined, but at one point or another he's also forked out for bench cloggers like £27m plodder Edin Džeko, square-jawed ball-squarer Gareth Barry and tenacious master-of-none James Milner. All three, along with many other expensively acquired fifth wheels, take home more money in thousands of pounds a week than they contribute in minutes on the pitch.

Liked Panini so much he decide to play for real. [3]

My mistake was to think that these were people like us. In fact, the kind of person who thinks sporting results should be as predictable as shopping trips probably sees players as objects, no different to a garage of sports cars.

Football is increasingly owned by two kinds of people: the heartless Randian businessmen, who think nothing exempt from the logic of profit, and the others who recognise no authority but their own needs. It's roughly equivalent to those who'd see no problem investing in an online human organ trading business and those who are already running on a black-market liver acquired from China.

Of course, good players aren't sports cars. They're a great deal rarer and less reliable, mostly one-offs or limited editions. At any one time, there are no more than a couple of dozen in Europe capable of giving you the edge. So if they're all parked in the same few garages, the race will tend to be less exciting, with fewer likely winners and an overall lower average speed.

---

3   As a seven-year-old, my pocket money allowed me to afford two packets of football stickers a week. For months a conclave of boys met in the playground every lunch break, rifling each other's spares and shouting 'got, got, got, got, need'. Until, one day, the resident rich kid got interested and his dad bought him a whole box from the village newsagent. He turned up the next day with a finished album and killed the whole game. As punishment, we refused to let him play British Bulldogs for a whole week, but the damage was already done...

At the end of July 2013, Betfair was offering odds of 750/1 or higher on 14 of the 20 Premier League clubs winning the 2013/14 title. In other words, without a ball being kicked, 70 per cent of the teams were deemed to have as close to no chance as makes no difference. Compare with the odds for the 2013/14 NFL season. Jacksonville, the bookies' lowest rated team in the entire league, were just 200/1 to win the Super Bowl. Twenty-six of the 32 teams had odds lower than 100/1.

The Premier League isn't yet a Scottish- or Spanish-style duopoly, where a long-running but no-longer-funny double act go through the motions, but the trend is clear (it's as though somehow Morecambe and Wise and The Two Ronnies mixed up, leaving Ernie Wise and Ronnie Corbett toiling joylessly round inner city Scotland in the winter, while Eric Morecambe and Ronnie Barker put on command performances in the more accommodating climate of Spain).

And it's not just the likelihood of your team winning the title that suffers. The greater the concentration of talent, the worse the overall standard of football. It can be entertaining occasionally to watch Chelsea whip Aston Villa 8-0, but great games of football – games worth watching for 90 minutes instead of a 90-second highlights package – have to involve two good teams. Which is why most Premier League games are now too tedious to watch live.

Particularly agonising are the teams in seventh or eighth. It's hard to believe – for all the money – how low the general level of technical ability is in squads that could, with a good run, qualify for a football lesson from a German team in next year's Europa League.

Even the 'big clubs' admit there's a problem, welcoming (publicly, at least) UEFA's Financial Fair Play regulations. It's a strange kind of fair play, though – and one that will do nothing to increase the likelihood of Swansea or Norwich ever winning the Premier League. Broadly, you aren't allowed to spend more

'Ready to fight?'

on wages than your total income. Which is like staging a race where everyone is limited to roughly the kind of car they have now. Nice if you're already driving a Ferrari. Not so good if you are in a Mondeo.

In 2011/12, Man City spent £202m on wages, which is more than four times as much as Blackburn, West Brom, Wigan, Wolves, Norwich or Swansea. Only six teams in the Premier League spent more than one third of the amount City did. The results are predictable, with a strong relationship over time between money spent on wages and final league position.

The problem is that, according *The Guardian*[1], no club in 2011/12 spent more than 100 per cent of its income on wages. Indeed, in descending order, the top ten were Blackburn, QPR, Villa, City, Bolton, Sunderland, Everton, Fulham, Stoke and West Brom. This might even suggest that Financial Fair Play will protect only larger clubs from themselves while encouraging ever greater risk-taking for smaller clubs (it's one thing to spend every penny and just miss out on the title. But spend all you have just to stay in the Premier League and *then* get relegated and it's hello, bankruptcy).

Here's the point: a meaningful limit on player wages has to be low enough that everyone can afford it and it has to be uniform.

Which is exactly how it is in the NFL. The NFL salary cap has remained pretty much static for the last five years, allowing teams to spend a maximum of about £77m ($120m USD) a year on wages.

It's not as much as it sounds. The £77m has to cover all 53 members of the roster. Shared equally, that would be about £28,000 a week per player. Halve the figure to reflect the fact that Premier League squads have a maximum of 25 players and it would translate to about £40m per Premier League team. The only clubs who spent less than that on wages in 2011/12 were Wigan, Wolves, Norwich and Swansea. And all would've been within touching distance of the NFL rule than mandates clubs *must* spend a minimum of about 90 per cent of their salary cap (a rule which stops owners profiting from fielding a cheap team).

When a salary cap is even and low, things suddenly become more interesting in a number of different ways.

In the 21 years of the Premier League to the end of the 2012/13 season, just five teams had won the title. A further three teams had finished second.[4] In the same period, 11 different teams won the Super Bowl with a further ten making a losing appearance. This includes two Super Bowl titles for Green Bay, a community-owned team from a town of just over 100,000 people. Michael MacCambridge, a brilliant US sports writer, asked former Green Bay club president Bob Harlan about the continuing success of the club. Despite all its great history and nationwide support, Harlan said, the team simply wouldn't be viable in Green Bay but for the salary cap and NFL profit sharing.[2]

The most important thing the salary cap accomplishes is not that it becomes impossible to try and acquire the league's best player, but rather that it becomes

---

4   In English football, the shrinking pool of winners seems to be a trend going back to the post-war restoration of the top flight. In the 1950s, six different teams won the title. In the 60s it was seven. This was followed by five in the 70s, four in both the 80s and 90s and just three in the 2000s.

impossible to have a star player at every position – let alone City's stated aim of having two for each position. If you want to sign a big name, you have to pay the rest a lot less.

'I like it. I'll take three.'

Simply put, then, a club can't buy the title (had a cap been present in English football for the last ten years, we may even have seen fewer teams sold to foreign owners with more money than patience).

A cap doesn't appear to penalise star players either. Quite the contrary, in fact: the ten best-paid players in the NFL for the 2014/15 season all accounted for more than $15m – or one seventh – of their teams' salary cap (which would be like City paying someone £900,000 a week[5]).

But it comes with risks. Peyton Manning, who some consider the greatest quarterback of all time, took Indianapolis to the play-offs (a marker of a good season, like qualifying for Europe) in 11 of his 13 years with the team. In 2011, with a squad built around him – and paying him the lion's share of the team's salary cap – Manning got injured and missed the entire season. Unable to afford a good back-up, Indianapolis won only two of 16 games. At the end of the year it wasn't just the head coach who got fired, it was the general manager too – the person, like a director of football, responsible for player recruitment and wages.

There are no creative workarounds for the salary cap either. You can re-structure contracts, bringing forward or pushing back bonuses and wages into different years, but the cap always catches up with you eventually, forcing you to cut or trade players to meet a year's number. And because salary caps are agreed several years in advance, with no provision for the aggressive wage inflation of

---

5   Note to anyone reading this book in 2018 or later: £900,000 a week would once have been considered an excessive amount of money for a football player to earn.

the Premier League, teams know that bargain hunting and coaching will always be the best long-term strategy.

Occasionally, if salary cap negotiations between the players and owners fail, there is an 'uncapped year'. The last time this happened was 2010, allowing, in theory, teams to go on spending sprees. One such team was Washington, who brought forward a proportion of their players' contracts, paying them in advance with the aim of hoarding talent for future years. But, so central to the NFL is the salary cap, this was deemed to be attempting to gain an unfair advantage so, despite the year having no salary cap, Washington were fined $36m.

Rather than pay from the owner's pocket, the team had that figure deducted from their next two years' salary caps – and then divided up among the rest of the teams in the league. In other words, in the NFL, instead of a fine that can be paid from a chairman's change jar, the punishment for over-spending on players is a direct cut in what you can spend in following years. Imagine the look on the face of the already perma-baffled Roman Abramovich if that had been Chelsea. In the Premier League clubs just don't hand down those kinds of punishments to each other.

'I'll have the biggest piece.' 'Me too.' 'And me.'

The salary cap has a pronounced sharpening effect on players too. In English football, if you're playing badly, you're just short-changing the owner and, to a lesser extent, the fans. In the NFL, you're robbing the team. There's no strolling through midweek cup ties or only turning up for big games. Every player has to justify his salary every week. If you don't – especially if someone is playing like a star and earning a new deal – you might be on the chopping block. Every contract a club hands out has an opportunity cost; every penny a player is paid is money that could've been used on other players.

Remember when John Terry was reported to have requested an 'unlimited parity' clause with Chelsea so that he'd always be the joint-highest paid player, regardless of what anyone else was earning? Good luck with that in the NFL. If you hit 30 and you aren't up to playing every game – and playing it brilliantly – your dodgy knees won't touch the ground on the way out of the door. Unless, that is, you're prepared to take a massive pay cut and play for the going rate. When did a Premier League player last do that?

Every plutocrat's starter superstar: Shaun Wright-Phillips (shown here at full size.)

Recently Baltimore, the 2012/13 Super Bowl champions, made their quarterback Joe Flacco the then best-paid player in NFL history, with a contact worth £80m over six years. The only way they could afford it was by letting seven other of their best players go and replacing them with youngsters. It would be like City winning their first title in years and then funding a huge new contract for Agüero by giving free transfers to Nasri, Kompany and Silva. A club like Chelsea might've been able to afford to add André Schürrle to their squad, but it's highly unlikely they'd also have been able to sign Diego Costa *and* get cover from an experienced player like Drogba. Compromises have to be made.

As I've said, top players still get paid for the difference they make. Which is as it should be. I've never minded how much Ronaldo gets paid; he earns every penny.[6]

---

6   Well, more precisely, Ronaldo is vastly, obscenely over-paid. But since he is a genuine once or twice in a generation talent, and clearly is a brilliant professional, I'm less bothered by it than the money mediocre players bring in. However, ultimately, all players – Ronaldo included – should be paid less.

What really began my alienation from football was when *decent* players or promising players or inconsistent ones got big pay days.

In the NFL, such players find their agents have much less leverage.

Recently, for example, Pittsburgh had two talented young wide receivers, Mike Wallace and Antonio Brown, coming to the end of their contracts. Each had shown great promise, leaving Pittsburgh in a situation that any Premier League club would be delighted by.

However, with the salary cap hanging over them and holes elsewhere on the team, Pittsburgh decided they could only afford to pay one of them. And, since neither player was yet excelling consistently, the team declined to offer top dollar, telling Wallace and Brown that there was one contract and it would go to the first player who signed.

Wallace, who at the time was considered the better player, held out for more money while Brown took the deal, getting $43m over six years. Wallace, meanwhile, was left to play out the last year of his contract on $2.7m before moving to a big money free agent deal with Miami.

Imagine that. Frank Lampard and John Terry come to the office, both wanting a new deal. But this time it's you sat behind the desk. You stand up, place a suitcase of money on the floor and look both players in the eyes. As you close the door behind you, you say, 'I only have one suitcase. I only expect one of you to come out of the room alive.'

And that's why a salary cap is brilliant: it frustrates the players, agents and trophy-hungry owners whose interest in pushing up salaries forces everyone else to join the Premier League's financial *danse macabre*.

It's a discipline that football desperately needs. Clubs' lives depend on it.

2.

'If that's not legal, I don't know what is...'

Because you can still tackle. Really hard.

I N American football there is an offence of 'unnecessary roughness'. Think about the implications of that for a moment: while 'unnecessary roughness' is to be abhorred, a certain amount of roughness is deemed an essential part of the game. The game is, by its very nature, violent. Wonderfully so, in fact.

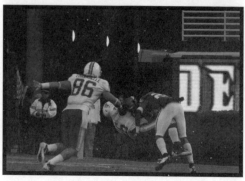

One is a foul. The other is not.

Most of my life as a football fan was spent watching lower-division football; brutal slogs on soggy bogs, where the chance of a serious injury seemed greater than that of a goal from open play.

In the early 1990s one of my team's midfield players – a fine string-puller but not a superstar – broke his leg. I was at his comeback over a year later. It was a home game, sparsely attended as they always were at the old ground.

It was an unusually warm and quiet day. So when, after only about 20 minutes, he went in for a 50-50 and broke his leg again – the same one in the same place – the whole ground heard it.

The sounds of a tibia snapping and of a grown man crying out in agony are not necessarily things I wish I could hear more often. But I do think football has lost its necessary roughness and is the worse for it.

Doubtless the players would disagree; I'm sure I would if I was out there playing for my livelihood every week.

But I'm not. I'm a sports fan who believes that certain sports, football included, demand an element of physical courage. This doesn't mean people have to get hurt for me to enjoy it, but there should be enough contact and aggression to make it at least a possibility (cricket lost its character with the introduction of the limit on bouncers. The sight of Brian Close facing the Windies without a chest guard or Viv Richards batting in a cap – daring England to try and hit him – was magnificent precisely because it was so foolhardy. Comparatively, it's now an international softball league).

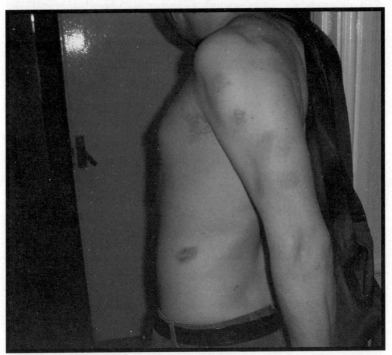

Brian Close, 'Hurt? I'm not a bloody footballer.'

It's often said that you don't need to watch a whole basketball game; you just come for the last five minutes to see who scores last. With the ever-decreasing levels of contact in the game, English football has become like basketball, just without the precision passing and reliable finishing. Teams ferry the ball rapidly and athletically from end to end before losing possession, meaning that, while you only need to watch five minutes of any game to see the important bits, you have no idea when those five minutes will be.

There's no better example of the dispiriting gentility of the game than the protection afforded to goalkeepers. Like pandas, those other undeserving beneficiaries of the global conservation movement, goalkeepers are a largely useless, permanently confused evolutionary dead end, unable either to fend for themselves or to adapt to the challenges presented by predators. And so they must be kept in a cage, with strikers unable to get within arm's length. At least pandas look cute (one has to wonder if small, tricky dribbling wingers are the football equivalent of the stag beetle: crucial to the maintenance of a healthy ecosystem but not cuddly enough to merit a pressure group).

Goalkeepers don't know how easy they have it, especially compared with what a quarterback has to handle. Now, granted, the two positions aren't directly equivalent. Goalkeeper is rarely regarded as the most important, most skilled position on a team, for example. And, in researching this piece, I could find no recorded instances of the fattest, least coordinated kid at school being 'stuck in' at quarterback.

Call to mind the outraged scowl of a keeper who's been lightly jostled by an opposition player running back and then read about Andrew Luck.

Andrew Luck: harder than a tungsten statue of Billy Bremner.[7]

---

7   The NFL is, of course, far from the only sport demanding ridiculous levels of physical endurance. By my reckoning, the Tour de France is the single hardest sporting event in the world. Mark Cavendish, the rocket-powered Manxman, has something of a reputation as a show-off among the sporting public. And yet cycling may be the only sport in the world where an athlete greets a dislocated shoulder, as Cavendish did, with, 'I'll see how it feels in the morning.'

Aged 23, he joined Indianapolis, the team that won only two of their 16 games in the 2011 season. Expected to immediately pick up and run a now decrepit team, directly after an all-time great had moved on, he somehow guided the side to 11 wins.

And he did it behind an offensive line so weak that he was knocked to the ground 148 times in a year, either while he was still holding the ball or directly after he'd thrown it.

And by knocked down, I don't mean one of those grand performances that keepers like to make when forced to bunny hop over an outstretched leg. This is being smashed, wrestled or thrown to the turf nine or more times a game by 18 stones of unsuppressed Joey Barton rage while you're trying to focus on throwing the ball with laser accuracy.

NFL players, you see, aren't wearing pads so it doesn't hurt. They're wearing them so they don't get killed. If you have five minutes to spare, put down this book, fire up YouTube and search for 'Andrew Luck + Nick Perry' to see the find of punishment a quarterback takes. Then search for 'Andrew Luck + Shareece Wright' to see how he deals it out.

Now imagine if the rules of football were changed so that goalkeepers were fair game when throwing or kicking the ball. Think how quickly they'd release the ball and how many miskicks would end up in the stands.

And it's not just quarterbacks who are under threat of violence. Almost every player will be involved in some kind of physical confrontation in every play of the game. Whether it's the big beasts wrestling on the line or a wide receiver getting drilled as he catches the ball, the game is played with continuous controlled fury.

Behold the following tackle. Search YouTube for 'Kam Chancellor legal hit'. San Francisco were playing Seattle in the NFC Championship game – effectively the Super Bowl semi-final. The San Francisco quarterback throws a high ball towards the corner of the field. A better pass here might've let the intended target catch it and sneak in for a touchdown. But it's a hospital pass; it hangs in the air, inviting a covering defender to take man and ball. San Francisco tight end Vernon Davis bravely goes up to catch it, keeping his eyes on the ball despite knowing he's going to get whacked by a Seattle player.

And get whacked he does. Seattle safety Kam Chancellor smashes into him, knocking the ball lose and Davis off the field. Even the toughest centre-back rarely tidied things up like this.

It's brutal to watch and it was actually given as a foul. Not because it was so hard it half-killed the opponent, but because Chancellor was deemed to have led with his helmet (if you intend to flatten someone in the NFL, the shoulder is the preferred body part with which to deliver the punishment). However, the replay and commentary suggest the referee got it wrong and that this was, in fact, a brilliant and completely legal piece of play. As commentator Cris Collinsworth muses watching the replay, 'If that's not legal, I don't know what is…'

Plays like this happen in every NFL game. But despite increased attention being paid to player safety, particularly the impact of cumulative head trauma, with this level of contact comes injuries, often horrendous. The attrition rate for players is frightening and the evidence is that the long-term consequences mentally and physically are unmerciful. It takes genuine courage just to pad up.

I wouldn't play the game for all the money in the world. But, god, is it magnificent.

Football, by contrast, is still hard, testing and powerfully contested, but it's no longer a game with a physical edge. No one misses the tackle from behind or the raised elbow, but the game has lost some of its necessary roughness – and it's the poorer for it.

3.

'Average footballer, excellent plumber...'

Because ex-players have to earn the right to manage.

THERE'S a saying, often attributed without evidence to Sun Tzu, that 'if you wait by the river long enough, the bodies of your enemies will float by'. In football the opposite is true. Wait long enough by the shabby banks of the Thames or the Trent or the Humber and eventually every one of your boyhood heroes will float past, dead or drowning under the weight of the lower-division club they're managing.

Should've opened a pub instead.

What do Tony Adams, Ray Wilkins, Alan Shearer, Peter Shilton, David Platt, Stuart Pearce and John Barnes have in common? Lots of correct answers, but the one I was thinking of was 'great players, crap managers'. And, more specifically, that each of them won more caps for England than they did league games as managers.

Other people you might expect to be on that list – Terry Butcher, Bryan Robson, Glenn Hoddle, and (non-Englishmen) Roy Keane and Mark Hughes – all managed for long enough to clock up the necessary face-saving wins. Paul Ince is the only player of that vintage and calibre with a managerial career (just), but it took him nearly seven years in and out of work to earn his 89 wins.

As a group, they weren't just wretchedly ill-equipped for the complexities of management. They were, sadly, so highly respected as players that a seemingly endless queue of chairmen went weak at the knees and awarded them one undeserved appointment after the next.

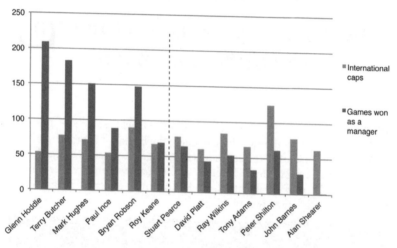

Strengths: kicking balls. Weaknesses: explaining things.[8]

As a football fan, there were two things I cared about: how my team was doing and the state of the game generally. The latter grows more important as you get older and see enough seasons to realise that nothing really changes, except slowly and for the worse. Football is a form of accelerated aging. The twilight drift into perpetual nostalgia hits football fans in their mid-30s, three decades ahead of the general population.

---

8   Figures correct as of the start of the 2013/14 season. Paul Ince has clocked up a few more wins since then and Mark Hughes continues to put teams out that play with the refined brutality he displayed on the pitch. The most interesting name on the chart, though, is Stuart Pearce who, back at Forest at the time of writing, may finally get to join 'The Guvnor' and other former England colleagues in boasting more managerial wins than international caps.

I no longer care who my club's next manager will be. But I'm still furious about when Mark McGhee walked out on us. I like our new young striker, but he's no Jimmy Quinn. And even if it turns out he's actually better, he still won't be the one who scored a glorious late winner in a 3-2 home victory over Plymouth in 1993.

So when I say that playing and managing should be treated as two completely different activities, my interest isn't purely academic. Yes, hiring a former player right out of retirement is footballing madness. But, worse than that, it contaminates our memories of them as players.

Gather round and throw on your winner's medals.

If only all former pros had the self-awareness of Andy Linighan, the former Arsenal centre-back turned tradesman, whose van supposedly carries a vinyl that reads, 'Average footballer, excellent plumber.'

For someone of my age, booing Bryan Robson – Captain Marvel! – was a sickening feeling, even as an opposition fan. I actually felt traumatised by it. I didn't want him looking ever more hangdog and frustrated as Boro's boss. It's like finding Audrey Hepburn, all aged and raddled, serving in the customer canteen in your local Debenhams. That's not how I want to remember him. Robson must never be allowed to age. He should be encased in carbonite, so he can live on in my memory – forever crashing around the England midfield, with that goal against France and that tragically spring-loaded shoulder.

We could've been spared it all – Tony Adams's literary quotations, Alan Shearer's 'I don't see myself as a number two' declaration, Mark Hughes's misguided resignation from Fulham, Stuart Pearce finally putting himself before his team when struggling with the Under-21s – if only the FA would step in and save players from themselves. Imprison them, deport them, stuff them and add them to the permanent collection of the British Museum. Whatever you do, just don't let them buy a whistle and a stopwatch.

That being a good player won't make you a good manager is obvious enough, but I wonder if we need to go further and demand the game actually invests in the idea of management – like refereeing – as a completely separate profession for which playing experience is not a necessary requirement.

It sounds crazy, except of course when you consider that there's already evidence that not being a player isn't a barrier to success. José Mourinho, André Villas-Boas and Brendan Rodgers never played a minute of professional football.

Bryan Robson preserved for the nation.

Others, like Roberto Martinez and Malky Mackay, have little or no experience of top-flight football.

Before we conclude, though, that football has already mended its ways – and that the era of top players being gifted a plum role has passed – it might be wise to give it a few years and see what offers are extended to Scholes, the Nevilles, Terry, Lampard, Gerrard et al.

And while we're waiting, let's take a look at the role of head coach in the NFL – a sport where they recognise that importing professionalism into sport means more than just trying to gouge more money from the fans.

At the start of the 2013/14 season, 23 of the 32 NFL head coaches – over 70 per cent – had never played a single game of professional football. And even those who had boasted a limited sporting CV. Together, that crop of coaches had an average two years' experience each as a player in the NFL.

And even that low figure is misleading, however, skewed as it is by five coaches who had NFL careers of nine years or more. Of those five, only three were good enough to play regularly and only one, Mike Munchak of Tennessee, had a career that would make Steve Bruce jealous.

So being a great player – or even a player at all – doesn't seem to be regarded as good preparation for management in some sports.

The really telling stat, however, is how long it takes to become an NFL head coach. On average, they had to work for 19.8 years before they got their first NFL head coach gig. That's right: because coaching is so difficult and

'It is exactly because a man cannot do a thing – like finding space in a crowded penalty area – that he is the proper judge of it.'

arduous a career, you have to learn and progress for nearly 20 years to get to the top of the tree.

And this is an average not skewed by outliers. Only two coaches got their first NFL job after less than ten years and the three best players still had to work for between 14 and 17 years after they retired to earn their spurs.

In the NFL, then, the vast majority of coaches had no professional career and even those who did tended to be plodders. Having been a player might trim a few years off the time it takes to become a coach, but it's still a massive long-term commitment.[9]

---

9   Even the designation 'coach' holds a certain weight that we don't impute to the term 'manager'. We'd never refer to someone as Manager Ferguson or Manager Wenger and you'd never hear a journalist yelling 'manager, manager!' in a post-match press conference. It's a job title, not a qualification. In the US, however, 'coach' is an honorific, a title that's retained even on retirement. Switch on an NFL broadcast and you may well see a roundtable discussion between people long out of the game all addressing each other as coach.

Michael MacCambridge suggests NFL coaching may now more complex and skilled than in any other sport and quotes Ernie Accorsi, a former general manager of the New York Giants, as saying that, while players are still the deciding factor, coaches are ever more important in determining the outcome of games.[3]

Which makes me think about a footballing cliché that would be astonishing if it were true. Can it really be right that, once the players cross the white line, there's nothing a manager can do? Is it true that you can't coach players, adjust formations without substitutions or respond to the opposition's performance without waiting for half-time?

Given the continued rise of the superstar coach in every sport from tennis to cycling, it seems odd to me that football managers should be unable to exert more influence on games. Perhaps we just aren't demanding enough of managers? Or perhaps we can't expect more of managers while they're drawn almost exclusively from the ranks of elite sportsmen?

As so often in American football, things are as they should be in a sport. The game is carefully administered to get the best coaches in jobs and protect the reputations of ex-pros – so that the adrenaline, exhilaration and intellectual challenges of the now don't perturb the precious memories of our sporting past.

The great players hobble off into the sunset to enjoy a retirement beset by arthritis, back problems and ruined knees, while fans can indulge their nostalgia, secure in the knowledge that even if a player felt to urge to sully his legacy, the career path of the coach would prevent it.

It's better for everyone that way.

'I can create the dishes, choose the linen, source the produce, and hire and train the staff – but, once the restaurant opens, there's nothing I can do.'

4.

'In goes Massing and, oh, he won't get past that challenge...'

Because there are no cups or internationals.

'IMAGINE no possession' wrote John Lennon in 1971, bemoaning Bobby Charlton's recent retirement from international football and its likely impact on the England midfield's ball retention. Nearly 40 years before the arrival of the Golden Generation, Lennon satirised the remorseless

One of the few times when Lennon's writing... [10]

---

10 One of the few times when Lennon's writing directly addressed his favourite sport, 'Imagine' was conceived as a riposte to McCartney's dreary paean to Liverpool's victorious 1965 FA Cup team, 'The Long and Winding Road (To Wembley)'. Piqued by what he took to be McCartney's bourgeois and condescending attitude to the song's dedicatee, Tommy Smith, Lennon instructed Phil Spector to rerecord the track's orchestral parts. It was a provocation too far for McCartney who quit the band, but not before he'd torched Yoko Ono's treasured Huddersfield Town away shirt.

commercial logic of the modern game, laying out how a concentration of wealth in the First Division would undermine other domestic competitions and ruin the England team.

Brought up by parents who regarded *Let It Be* as the best Beatles album, I wasn't exposed to Lennon's message until my early teens. Even then, for me, the gap between knowledge and understanding was nearly 20 years.

My favourite World Cups were Mexico 86 and Italia 90. These were magical, innocent times. Unencumbered by cynicism, my friends and I revelled in England's heroic exits from tournaments that supplied an almost never-ending list of wonderful football moments. In the playground we passed like Platini, dribbled like Maradona, dived like Klinsmann, stepped-over like Waddle, fouled like Massing, scissor-kicked like Negrete and finished like Careca.

The lost magic of the World Cup: Massing goes in on Klinsi.

It was only in 2010, five World Cups later, that I realised that I hadn't actually enjoyed a World Cup since the days of Beardsley and Lineker. Twenty years of disappointing England performances had just taken all the joy out of it (even 1994, where I watched every match for evidence of how far we might have got had we qualified).

It's the same for domestic cup competitions. If the Premier League and the England team aren't prepared to take games seriously, then neither am I. The Premier League's obvious disregard for non-Premier games is a poison that's spread further down the pyramid. In the Championship, FA Cup third round day triggers a Dutch auction with table-topping managers competing in a Putinesque show of manliness to see who can field the weakest team and still win.

Mick McCarthy names his FA Cup first 11, 'One starter, three subs, a youth teamer, a shop dummy, a Sunday League ringer, a Rasputin puppet, a samovar, a wolfhound and a 70ft concrete statue of Stalin.'

Popular wisdom holds that Manchester United killed the FA Cup by ducking out of the 1999/2000 competition. A dubious notion, at best. To my mind, the stake was driven into its heart at the end of the 96/97 season when, for the first time, the Premier League was invited to provide two entries for the following year's Champions League.

TV money, which was already marginalising domestic competition in England, dictated that the reshaped European Cup needed a guaranteed contingent of big names every year. From then on the only victories with value were those that pushed teams up the league and towards greater financial rewards. Everything else – the Charity Shield, the Zenith Data Systems Cup, the Anglo-Italian Cup, the Cup Winners' Cup – was cancelled, rebranded or left to wither. Right now the League Cup and the Europa League (UEFA Cup, as was) are on life support.

In the NFL they keep things simple. There are four pre-season friendlies and a 16-game season that leads to the play-offs. There is only one competition and only one prize: the Super Bowl. Everything else – divisional wins, play-off wins, conference wins – are simply a measure of progress towards what must be the end goal for all teams. At the end of the season, there is one winner and 31 losers.

It's this kind of radical honesty that football fans, locked in a loveless marriage with clubs and players who barely recognise their existence, desperately need. In fact, let's go further. There's just too much football full stop.

'Imagine there's no countries, it isn't hard to do. Nothing to kill or die for, and no League Cup too.'

Last season, including friendlies and cup games, England's top teams played over 60 games. With that many they can't all be equally important to players or fans. And even if they were, where would you find the time and money just to make it to all the home games?

In 2012/13, Super Bowl winners Baltimore played 20 competitive games and four friendlies. Attending the home games and play-offs committed you to a maximum of just 12 games.

Fewer games and no extraneous competitions gives fans the luxury of seeing a good chunk of their team's matches without having to resign from their job or their family. For players and coaches, though, it creates an almost stifling shortage of opportunities to prove themselves. As a consequence, there is a pronounced edge to every fixture.

The only novelty in the calendar is the Pro Bowl. An annual all-star exhibition match where players compete for either the NFC or AFC (the two, largely arbitrary, halves of the NFL), the game's value lies in the recognition it gives those chosen. It's as if the PFA selected two teams of the year and then staged a training game. The problem is, with so few competitive games in a year, players are less and less willing to risk getting hurt. As a consequence, the Pro Bowl has become a viewing spectacle on par with Soccer Aid, but without the excitement of someone fouling a pop star.

The NFL's response, in a last-ditch effort to save the game, has been to revive one of the most primal aspect of playground sports. Instead of being voted on to the NFC or AFC team, all the players will be pooled and the captains will take turns to pick.

It won't work, but I like where they're coming from.

Meanwhile English football continues to squeeze every last drop of milk from the game's exhausted udders, stuffing the calendar with ever more fixtures, unable and unwilling to recognise the need to provide competitive, affordable, high quality sport to its fans.

But would I really want an end to the England international team? Well, either that or they agree to play properly and stop spoiling the World Cup for me.

Your choice, FA.

5.

'John Williams, a former postman from Swansea...'
Because you can prove you're right.

YESTERDAY I had 6.7 hours of sleep, consumed 2,781 calories, produced 1.32 litres of urine, coughed up 2.4 grams of sputum, experienced 79 minutes of deep concentration, scratched my knee four times and was indisputably correct once about who Reading's greatest ever midfielder was. Isn't Big Data amazing?

Of course, not all of the above is true. I know – I absolutely know – Simon Osborn was Reading's most gifted centre-mid of all time. But despite my FuelBand, pedometer, wireless pacemaker, subcutaneous GPS implant and Google Glass, I just can't prove it.

In the old days this was good. That football wasn't and could never be susceptible to statistical analysis was an article of faith for fans and evidence of its inherent superiority to other sports, especially silly American ones involving pads. Only nerds liked numbers and computers, while real men liked beer and Formula 1.

But recently computers have done quite well for themselves and now we're all eager to proclaim our inner nerddom. Men who would previously engage with the idea of measurement only in the context of putting up shelves will now happily plot a map of their recent mountain bike ride and upload it for the edification of their friends. Even George Osborne, a man previously so contemptuous of physical activity that he has a footman to open the sports cap on his water-bottle, has come out as being into the quantified self.

So, after only ten millennia of being comfortable with simply asserting the truth of a claim, many sports have recently entered that 17th century with the recognition that it might be possible – and even worthwhile – to actually be able to prove things.

Not even the best Osborn(e) in this chapter: the chancellor with his FuelBand.

Football, sadly, isn't quite there yet. Clubs measure their players with Prozone and Opta have their stats but it's largely away from the public's eyes. In the 1990s, a cabal of football journalists, worried about the impending requirement to go beyond producing vague and impressionistic match reports using NUJ-approved templates, managed to discredit the use of stats by introducing the concept of 'assists'. This false flag operation set the cause of evidence in football back 25 years by presenting to the public something that, one, had more holes in it than Kevin Keegan's Newcastle defence and, two, sounded American.

Which is why, if I ask you who the fastest player in the Premier League is, you're perfectly entitled to claim it's Aaron Lennon or Raheem Sterling or Theo Walcott. You can even maintain, if you really want to, and against the derision of your audience, that it's Per Mertesacker. And no one can tell you any different. It is, after all, a game of opinions (I once met a football fan who claimed David Beckham was rubbish at football – not 'sub-world class', but actually rubbish – because the fan had once played schoolboy football with former Irish international Alan Kernaghan and he therefore *knew* what he was talking about).

Ask an NFL fan the fastest player question and they can tell you that, with a time of 4.24 seconds, Chris Johnson of the New York Jets recorded the fastest 40-yard dash of any current player coming out of college. He may not be the fastest now, knocking on 30 and with his performances tailing off, but it gives you at least some anchor for discussion. You could also resolve who's the strongest, the cleverest, who can jump the furthest and a dozen other characteristics without ever having to have dribbled round a future Middlesbrough centre-half.[11]

The nearest we got in football to this level of player data was the Rumbelows Sprint Challenge. Here Reading got dangerously close to actually winning something, with our greatest ever left-winger (fact), Michael Gilkes, being pipped at the post by Coventry's John Williams.

Michael Gilkes in his pomp.

Even then it was a typically half-arsed football effort. If you measure the wrong thing, even if you do so accurately, you're liable to mislead. You can see it in the Champions League games where substitutions are often accompanied with a stat showing how far a player ran.

---

11   The intelligence test is called the Wonderlic test. It's a 50-question multiple choice test lasting 12 minutes. While there's plenty of room for dispute about the value of such a test – what exactly do we mean by 'intelligence'? Is it the same thing that the Wonderlic measures? And how relevant is intelligence to future sporting performance anyway? – it's fascinating because the decades of testing allow us to see what positions tend to produce the highest scores. Typically it's offensive linemen, the oft-mocked fat guys in the trenches. who score best – which goes some way to showing the complexity of a job that, at first glance, looks like synchronised nightclub bouncing. Of course, if we had had the Wonderlic in the Premier League, we'd know for sure if Graeme Le Saux really was the first clever football player in history and if midfield schemers actually can outsmart clogging centre-backs. It might also lead us to adopt other standardised ways of measuring valued player attributes. I'd be interested to see, for example, whose left foot could actually open the most tins of peas, Gareth Bale's or Cristiano Ronaldo's, and if Bale's is, as I suspect, the more cultured, despite Ronaldo's having its own museum.

As someone whose footballing career was characterised by running around hopefully but slowly after the ball, I can be certain (completely certain) that distance covered may tell you something about effort expended but little else. When pundits talk about the importance of movement, they mean something like 'being in the right place at the right time to make the right run to help your team accomplish what it needs to do at a given moment'. Reporting on how far someone has run is therefore about as useful as reporting on how many times a player has kicked the ball.

In the case of the Rumbelows Sprint Challenge, the organisers came up with the idea of racing over 100m – only slightly shorter than the whole length of a typical professional football pitch. The last time a player was motivated to run that far it was Emmanuel Adebayor celebrating the beginning of the end of his career.

In the NFL, they measure players over 40 yards. That tells you about what's more important than speed: acceleration. Which is why – because Gilkes was leading for the first half of the race – I can know (and it's real unshakable knowledge) that he was the quickest lower-league footballer of his generation.

What few stats football does now grudgingly produce are shot through with the same half-witted approach to measurement. How many corners equal one goal, for example? Well, if Reading are taking them, very few. And yet 'corners won' is reported as though it's a useful proxy for being likely to score; as if, like houses in Monopoly becoming hotels, corners will convert at a high and known rate into goals.

Only 30 metres and 11 players stand between us and our inevitable goal.

Worse is football's headline stat: shots on target. Whether applied at a club or player level, it tells you little of use. To be worthwhile, it would have to at least exclude the shots that required only a simple save from the keeper. To not do that is to suggest that goalkeepers and strikers aren't really part of the game and any contribution they make is essentially a bonus. What's required then is a measure of quality goalscoring opportunities created by a team or player, rather than how often an over-eager striker scuffed a speculative shot on the turn.

But is such a thing possible? Ask the NFL.

Beneath every headline statistic is a myriad of illuminating sub-categories that help you tease out just how well someone is playing. In football, we can find out what percentage of a player's passes were completed. Which is nice if all you do is play lots of short square passes to players with a good first touch. But what about if you're a player whose job it is to open up a defence or spread the ball?

In the NFL, the quarterback, who throws 99.5 per cent of his team's passes, has a headline pass completion rate. Behind that, though, the journalists will report how many of those passes were catchable – ie, those where his team-mate dropped the ball and those where he actually threw the ball badly.

He'll also be measured on the average distance each pass travelled and the average distance the ball was advanced downfield after the catch was made. This will show how much was the contribution of the quarterback and how much the person who caught it. This means players with a lower completion rate who are throwing longer (and therefore harder to complete) passes can be recognised. A bit more sophisticated than assists, no?

In American football, credit is also given if a player is under pressure. The stats note how often the quarterback has time to pass unhindered by opposition players getting in his face and how often he's trying to make a throw while a 20-stone brute is making his life flash before his eyes. In football, this would be like giving extra credit to Messi for constantly playing while having his ankles nipped at or to Matt Le Tissier for carrying the burden of being the only good player on a bad team.

What underlies all this is, I think (though I'm unable to be sure) a different, more reverential and humble attitude toward American football and the game's complexity from its fans. While there are many fewer games, each game is vastly more involved. Football's wonderful fluidity and lack of rules, combined with the sheer volume of games, is apt (I think I can say with some confidence) to induce laziness and sloppy thinking in fans.

What passes for debate between football fans is often just an elaborate parlour game in which grown men take turns to name football players they may have seen play once or twice and say if they are good or bad. The next person will critique the previous person's contribution, which amounted to little more than a list of players they like or don't like, by saying if they like or don't like the players. They will then embellish the round by listing other players they either do or don't like. This continues until finally someone names a player that everyone can agree they all like (or dislike). Xavi or Stewart Downing, for example.

In essence, most discussion of football – even from professionals in paid media – is largely devoid of information. Rather a narrative for the game is created, often based around a supposedly telling incident – a goal, a mistake, a sending-off – with a player or manager cast in the central role.

'My favourite colour is green.' 'You're an idiot, mate, yellow is much better.'

The lack of analytical rigour that football breeds – and its boneheaded rejection of statistics as a means of illuminating the game – is embedded in the whole way even foundational aspects of the game are described. If, for example, you are getting soundly beaten and, with five minutes left, score a goal to make it 3–1, you've got what is known as a 'consolation'. Except it doesn't make anyone feel any better. Just ask Oscar, scorer of perhaps the least consoling goal in history, who despite netting in the final minute of Brazil's epic 7-1 defeat to Germany in the World Cup, promptly burst into tears when the final whistle blew.

In the NFL, where an act's value is measured in relation to the game, Oscar would've scored in what is known as 'garbage time'. It's there on the scoreboard, but everyone knows that a late score when the game has already been decided is much less important than one early when there's all to play for.

In the US, this notion of making it count is critical. They measure teams and quarterbacks by their likelihood of scoring once they are close to the opposition goal line. Reliability in this 'red zone' is critical since it speaks to efficiency, coaching and a winning mindset. Likewise a wide receiver who can be relied upon to get open and make catches in the endzone, when the ability to make a catch is never harder nor more valuable, will be esteemed more highly than other receivers. A running back who's good at moving the ball late in the game, allowing his team to run down the clock and keep the ball away from the opposition, is called a 'closer'. A quarterback with a high number of 'fourth quarter comebacks' – Roy Keane's never-say-die ability to bring the ball out of defence and drive the team on to a late winner – is given the ultimate accolade: a 'clutch' player.

The names are awkward, but the NFL has found a way to produce stats that show which players make a difference. How much better if football debate was more often seasoned by facts about who finishes under pressure, who tackles cleanly in the box late in the game and who can be relied upon to score the winner on the break? Instinctively we all know this is what counts, we just don't have the proof. And sadly, most of the time, we don't even want it. Why would we? We already know what we think; we don't need evidence to muddy the water.

Is this the greatest free-kick taker in history?[12]

---

12 Ask enough people who the best dead-ball specialist in history was and Roberto Carlos will poll well, largely because of THAT goal. And while kicking it hard – really hard! – is thrilling, I always marvelled at how many shots he smashed wildly over the bar (if only someone could compare his goals per free kick average with other great free-kick takers, factoring in the distance and difficulty of the ball position, and find a way of marking him down for all the long-range efforts he might have been better using as the start of an attack). My strong belief – in the absence of the numbers – is that teams with Roberto Carlos in probably made less of their dead-ball situations than teams with, say, Mihaojlovic or Beckham in. Statistical analysis has proved particularly valuable in the NFL for assessing what decision a coach should make on fourth downs. This is the situation where a team must either try and move the ball a set distance forward or risk losing it to the opposition. Depending on the field position, a coach who doesn't think his team can reach the first down marker may elect to kick a field goal, worth three points, or, if they are too far away, punt the ball. This is the equivalent of the goal kick, surrendering the ball to the opposition, albeit further down the pitch. More innovative coaches have compared data from thousands of previous games and recognised that, in certain field positions, the odds of risking a fourth down failure are still better than the expected outcome of punting the ball back to the opposition. One college coach famously *never* punts the ball. He'd always rather try and hold on to the ball and risk losing it closer to his goal line than guarantee giving the ball to the opposition back in their half. Why is this relevant? Well, imagine that we could analyse free kicks closely, so that, with the position, distance, angle, number of players in the wall, ability of the goalkeeper etc, we could compare the expected outcome of shooting – goal, goal kick, save, corner etc – and determine if there were a whole class of situations when taking quick free kicks or simply not shooting and aiming instead to retain possession might be, on average, a more advantageous tactic.

Me, I love stats.

Sometimes they can help clarify something you already knew. When Ferguson retired, I spoke to some Chelsea fans who claimed he was a great manager but wasn't as dominant as the write-ups of his career suggested. It's hard to overstate how wrong this is. In his 21 seasons in the Premier League, United won the title on 13 occasions (62 per cent). They finished in the top two on 18 of 21 occasions (88 per cent) and never outside the top three. With the exception of the three seasons from 2003/04 to 2005/06, Manchester United fans never went more than a year without a title to celebrate.

Nom nom nom. Lovely stats.

Sometimes they can overturn what you thought you knew. According to Squawka's 2012/13 stats:

- Leighton Baines created more goalscoring opportunities than Messi and Ronaldo combined.
- Xavi completed a pass every 50 seconds, while Michael Carrick completed more forward passes than any other player in Europe.
- Miroslav Klose had the highest conversion rate of any striker with more than 15 goals – just shy of four in every ten shots went in.[4]

Delicious.

At other times stats can help lay the groundwork for a debate. For example: more Jamaican discus throwers were been caught using performance enhancing drugs in 2013 than were players in the entire history of the Premier League. Conclusion? That cheating is less common in team sports? Well, more than 20 NFL players were caught in the 12 months to August 2013. That cheating is more common in games requiring explosive effort? Ask cycling fans. In the last 16 years, 12 of the 25 riders who finished in the top three in the Tour de France have been caught using drugs or have 'fessed up to it. Is testing in football not rigorous enough? Is the game actually clean? You tell me.

When I put the case for data, it's sometimes suggested that an NFL-style influx of stats would fragment our understanding of the game, creating more complexity than we can cope with. I can't see it. Big Data is a misnomer. What technology gives us is not merely the capacity to gather more data than ever but to analyse is; the power to understand and make sense of it.

For example, in 2011, in an effort to unify categories and make it possible to compare the performance of quarterbacks, ESPN developed the 'Total Quarterback Rating' (QBR). Supposedly composed of more than 10,000 lines of code, the QBR gives a single number to measure the contribution of a quarterback to every one of his team's plays, based on how difficult it was and its impact on the final score. Likewise, there are metrics to measure a defence's performance against both passing and running plays as well as their reciprocal: metrics to measure an offense's performance when running or passing the ball.

None of these are perfect and they don't end the debate. Nor, crucially, do they seem to take the magic out of the game. What it does do, though, is inform and enable it (I'm pretty sure of this).

Imagine if football was so well measured, the data so well interrogated and, crucially, the insight woven into the fabric of how we all discuss football – rather than, as it is now, a nascent but still-peripheral art practised by some remarkable pioneers.

We could have more and better conversations. Conversations that taught us more than who someone's favourite player is. Conversations that didn't simply degenerate into nostalgia and historical one-upmanship. Conversations that kept sportswriters honest. Conversations that actually honoured the majesty of the sports to which we dedicate so much time and passion by helping us become expert analysts, instead of mere bar-room bores.

Above all, conversations that helped prove me right…

6.

'Who are they?' 'Exactly...'
Because one good season won't set you up for life.

GOOGLE 'the world's luckiest man' and you'll be directed to Frano Selak, a man who supposedly survived seven transport accidents that claimed a total of 40 lives before becoming a lottery winner with his first ever ticket. After Frano, in joint second place, is every British man born after 1980 with a modicum of football talent. Not only did they get to fulfil our childhood dream of being a professional footballer, but they got minted – even if it turned out they weren't all that good in the end.

Men like Francis Jeffers who in 2001, aged only 20, was signed by Arsenal for £8m after just 49 games for Everton. His reported basic salary was £35k a week – just less than £2m a year. He made just 22 league appearances, scoring only four goals.

Frano Selak, 'I survived a plane crash, a train derailment, two bus smashes and three car accidents. Last time I go out with Mario Balotelli.'

Or men like Shaun Wright-Phillips. Now past 30, he's made a little over 450 club appearances in his first 14 years in football – a few more than 30 games a season. Towards the end of his time at Manchester City, he was reportedly unhappy to be offered a bump from £60k a week to £70k, believing himself to be worth £100k. If you assume he's averaged £50k a week for the last ten years, then, conservatively, he's earned a basic salary of £26m over the course of his quite forgettable career. That's a lot of money for someone who couldn't truthfully be said ever to have excelled at football.

But this isn't a story of overpaid footballers. It's about something much more corrosive: young players getting big money the first time they flash a bit of skill. Andy Carroll. Scott Sinclair. Jermaine Pennant. Chris Smalling. The list goes on and on. Sometimes, like Daniel Sturridge or Jordan Henderson, they belatedly begin to perform to the level they are remunerated to. Either way, like gas bills, football wages are sticky upwards – they rise rapidly but are slow to come down.

Depending on which paper you read, Alex Oxlade-Chamberlain was on £60k a week in 2013/14 – a sum neither I nor the majority of British people have ever earned in a year. He was 20 and had played a full 90 minutes in the league *only once* the previous year. Is he a talented player? Undoubtedly. Should he have been paid more than three million quid a year before he'd even earned a regular place? You tell me.

American football used to have this problem. The contracts given to the top prospects coming out of college were spiralling, with tens of millions of dollars being lavished on players who'd yet to accomplish anything professionally.

A good example is the first player taken in the 2009 draft, Matthew Stafford. After four largely disappointing seasons in the league, the quarterback signed a $53m, three-year contract extension with Detroit. If he plays that out and hits his targets, he'll have earned more than £80m (or £172k a week for nine years). Even Shaun Wright-Phillips's agent might blush at that for a player who's been more Steven Pienaar than Steven Gerrard.

Matthew Stafford: owns a life-sized replica of Fort Knox entirely made of gold.

And so, facing ever greater demands from young players, the league introduced 'rookie contracts', governing the maximum players could get in their first four years in the league. The chart below shows the contract value of the highest paid young player in each of the last eight years. See if you can spot when the new contracts came in.

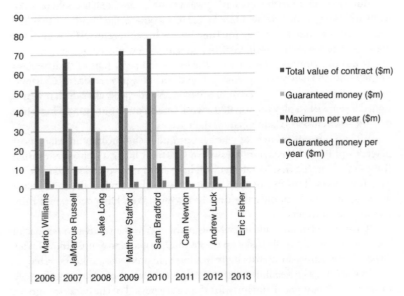

Contract values for the first overall draft picks.

It's simple, decisive action like this that means that, while Matthew Stafford and Sam Bradford may yet exceed Premier League footballers in the undeserved riches category, Cam Newton and those that follow him will have to earn their money. Outside of a few quarterbacks who slump after signing massive, multi-year deals, it's almost unknown in the NFL for journeymen players to retire as rich men who count their wealth in the tens of millions. It is possible to have a long career if you are prepared to pay for a modest salary, but the only way to get paid consistently well is to be consistently brilliant.

Essentially, under the new scheme, all players drafted out of college sign a four-year deal with a maximum and minimum value according to how high they were taken in the draft. The impact has been immediate in reducing young players' income and rebalancing how money is allocated across teams.

Take Robert Griffin III, who was drafted second overall in 2012 behind Andrew Luck (a phenomenal but orthodox player whose first few years in the NFL have already convinced people that he can become an all-time great). Griffin, meanwhile, (or RG3, as he is known) was an even more intriguing prospect to many. Possessed of awesome physical gifts (at one point in college he was the fifth fastest 110m hurdler in his age group in the world), he was so quick and so nimble that, no matter how quickly the defence got after him, he seemed able to elude them until either a receiver became open for him to pass to or he decided to zig-zag his way upfield, avoiding defensive attempts to smash him to pieces (historically, quarterbacks' importance mean they have usually been encouraged to run with the ball about as often as centre-backs are instructed by their managers to dribble the ball out of a crowded penalty area using their wrong foot).

But what made Griffin so exciting wasn't just his engine. He could pass the ball with remarkable finesse. Here at last was a quarterback with an arm like a laser and legs like a gazelle. YouTube one of his college or NFL highlights packages and see for yourself. Griffin had it all; a new player archetype.

It was like finding a player with the brain and right foot of Paul Scholes in the body of Theo Walcott. And yet, with the new pay structure, Griffin – perhaps the most exciting new sportsperson to emerge in the US that year – signed a contract to play for £67,000 a week for the next four years. This is like getting Neymar on Oxlade-Chamberlain wages.

It's still a lot of money, of course, but under the rookie contracts most players will be on considerably less than Griffin. Of the 256 players drafted this year, all but the first 32 selected will have contracts worth less than $6.5m over four years. This means the vast majority will be on less than £20,000 a week. And even then, only the first 18 players taken have negotiated fully guaranteed contracts.

'Guaranteed money' and its evil cousin, the 'offset' clause, are two wonderful concepts that would really shake up the Premier League and give Gordon Taylor (who will be featured unflatteringly in a later chapter) a brain haemorrhage.

In the NFL, the headline figure quoted for the value of contracts is largely misleading. If you play brilliantly for the entire period of the contract and hit all your targets, you'll get the money. But almost no one does that.

Because injury or declining performance could mean that you get cut – effectively given a free transfer – at any time, the only money you can be certain of getting is what's known as the guaranteed amount. Short of refusing to play or being sent to prison, nothing can stop you getting it.[13]

---

13 Not strictly true. Stupidity can also stop you. Because, if you get yourself suspended, the unpaid guaranteed amount remaining on your contract is voided. For a minor offence a team may not make an issue of it, but, if you are on the cusp of being too expensive, you can find bad discipline rapidly becomes bad financial management. In November 2013, for example, Kansas City wide receiver Dwayne Bowe smoked what could have been the most expensive joint in history. Suspended for one game for being arrested with a bag of marijuana, Bowe voided his entitlement to $10m of guaranteed money. There had already been rumblings that the last years of his contract with Kansas City would be poor value, paying him top ten wide receiver money for middling performance. Until that point, however, the guarantees in Bowe's contract meant Kansas City would have to pay him and the money would be deducted from their salary cap – leaving them short elsewhere. However, with his guarantees voided, Kansas City could afford to cut him – or demand he renegotiate and play for a salary that better reflected his performances. In the space of one traffic stop, he went from being too expensive to cut to too expensive not to cut.

Even then, if you are cut, your contract will often include an offset clause. This means that, if you sign with another team, the guaranteed money you're owed is deducted from your new salary. You won't, in other words, get your guaranteed money *and* your salary from your new club. There is no double dipping allowed in the NFL.[14] Only the very very top players can insist on a high percentage of the contract being guaranteed and no offsets, effectively making them too expensive to drop. Everybody else has to produce the goods.

Imagine your favourite scene from Seinfeld here.

The opposite is the case in football where the headline figure (still given, strangely, in pounds per week, as if it were for casual work in a mill) is in fact both the base salary and a fully guaranteed amount (unless you do a Mutu and get fired).

Football contracts are one-way bets. If he plays badly and turns out to be the next Vela rather than the next Kanu, Oxlade-Chamberlain will still get his full £15m-plus over five years. But if he plays well, two years from now, his agent will demand a new and even more lucrative contract.

It's these stupidly generous, fully guaranteed contracts that explain why many clubs struggle under the weight of squad player salaries – or have to send players on loan *and* still pay part of their wages. It's also why, if you're really cussed – like Winston Bogarde – and you refuse to take a pay cut to smooth

---

14 There is another situation, other than through contractual muscle, where double dipping is possible. When a player is cut, he goes on what's called the 'waiver wire' – the NFL transfer list. Effectively, his name is circulated to the other teams in the NFL along with details of his contract. If teams want him and can afford him, they put in a claim for him. Claims are considered, like the draft, with the worst team from the previous season getting first dibs. If a team gets a player, they then pick up his contract, relieving his previous team of their obligation to him. However, if a player 'clears waivers' and no team puts in a bid for him, he becomes a free agent – able to negotiate a new contract with any team that might want him. In this case he receives the remaining guaranteed money on his previous contract in full plus whatever his new team are prepared to pay him on the open market. Result.

a transfer away from the club, you can train with the kids for three years and still get £40,000 a week.

You might have thought that having to live with a contract would be good discipline for a club, but in the absence of a salary cap it doesn't appear to be. All it seems to do is to inflate salaries and take the edge off the requirement to play hard for young and old players alike.

In the world of work, you'll often be told that to get a promotion or a pay rise you have to first be doing the job you want to get paid for. Somehow, in the Premier League, you have only to show the merest hint of promise and a new contract will magically appear.

I don't say sportsmen shouldn't be paid well. It's a career that, with skill and dedication, can bring enjoyment, sometimes joy, to millions. It's also a short career and, compared to most others, a largely meritocratic one. But it really isn't right that so many young players become overnight millionaires when they've hardly even begun to master their craft, let alone proved their long-term worth. The people who should be the ultimate working class heroes – who, when they wear the shirt, embody our childhood dreams – have become, like the hated City bankers and expense-diddling politicians, totems of Britain's shameless, unfettered greed.

For a vision of a different way – where the value of player contracts, like all other investments, can go down as well as up – we return to Washington and their quarterback phenom Robert Griffin III.

Having mortgaged their future for RG3 by trading numerous draft picks for him, the team found they snagged a young player of prodigious talent and promise who also seems, sadly, to be injury prone and struggling to adjust to the demands of leadership.

Towards the end of a breathtaking first season, Griffin hurt his knee and, returning too soon for a play-off game, damaged two ligaments. His second season was a catastrophe, with Griffin looking a shadow of his previous quicksilver self and subject to frequent criticism from the press, fans and his coach for his attitude. The coach was fired at the end of the year and a new one brought in to 'fix' Griffin. As I write, two-thirds of the way through Griffin's third season, he's been hurt again, played dreadfully, and fallen out with a number of team-mates *and* his second coach. It's been a disaster for Washington, but, thanks to the rookie contracts set-up, not a financially ruinous one.

Griffin is far too talented to write off at this stage. But, if they choose to, Washington could walk away from him, content that they paid him well, but not excessively for the promise he showed but hasn't delivered. If it happens, he'll have to work his way back at a different team with the going rate for a perceived 'draft bust'. Andrew Luck, meanwhile, the man picked ahead of him, is coming towards the end of his third immaculate season. Sometime next year he will likely sign a new contract that will put him among the top five best paid players in the NFL. And he will have earned it.

As a postscript, Frano Selak, a man who acquired his money rather later in life, was reported to have given most of his lottery win away on the basis that 'money can't buy you happiness'. Francis Jeffers, meanwhile, finished last season playing for Accrington Stanley.

7.

'It just gets everybody to slow down... open their mind.'

Because they don't pretend racism is someone else's problem.

RACISM, like Luis Suarez's dental chart, is an ugly thing – and one that, like Gary Lineker's tenure on *Match of the Day*, seems remarkably and unwelcomely persistent.

In recent years there's been such a focus on racism on the pitch that attention has drifted, like Titus Bramble's concentration late in the game, away from racism in the boardroom.

So here's something to remember when next an FA spokesman, reading from a prepared statement, reasserts his organisation's commitment to rid the game of racism: there are more black men sitting in the House of Lords than there are managing English football teams. Indeed, as the appointment of Malky Mackay by Wigan has shown, a black man can find it harder to get hired as a football manager than someone being investigated for allegedly sending racially offensive text messages at work.

There's a particularly dispiriting line of defeatist thinking in Britain at the moment that runs: [X bad thing is happening], but no one's ever going to do anything about it. X can be, 'bankers are ruining Britain', 'the NHS is going to be destroyed despite being really quite popular', 'all global sporting bodies are horrendously corrupt' – the list of pub topics goes on. The lack of ethnic minority managers in English football is one such problem. Everyone recognises it, yet no one can conceive of anything being done about it.

Football fans, like British people generally, have given up fighting for their values. In place of hope and energy has come apathy and cynicism. What are you going to do, asks the sceptic, force teams to hire black managers?

No, we might reply, but perhaps we could consider doing something from the middle ground that must surely exist between mandating their hiring and

One day science will confirm that there is a direct line that leads from diving, through racism and eventually to cannibalism.

just carrying on doing diddly squat? Can we at least agree that the current disgraceful situation can't be allowed to continue?

I'm amazed at how hearteningly angry fans get when a young England player is racially abused abroad, yet how unconcerned they are about the fact that, at the beginning of the 2013 season, there was only one British ethnic minority manager in the Premier League (Chris Hughton). That's one of 20 – or just five per cent (this compared with eight white non-British managers in the Premier League). In the Championship, at the same time, there was Paul Ince and Chris Powell. And, in League 1 and League 2, where 96 per cent of managers were British, only one, Chris Kiwomya at Notts County, was from an ethnic minority. So, across the top four divisions of the English professional game, only four managers – about four per cent – were from ethnic minorities. All would subsequently get fired and, for a period, England would have no black managers.

House of Lords: surprising bastion of diversity.

This is a staggering under-representation when you consider that around 30 per cent of players in the top four divisions are non-white.[5] As I've noted in chapter three, football draws its managers almost exclusively from the ranks of former players, so it's hard to see how the current arrangement can be justified. The FA and the Premier League appear to think on-field racism is a problem, meting out good, strong punishment to high-profile players like John Terry and Luis Suarez. So why then so little interest in tackling other issues of equality?

Things have not always been better in the US. NFL writer Michael MacCambridge has documented how laws against mixed-race sport meant that, even in the 1950s, teams had to leave black players behind when competing in Florida. Yes, in my parents' lifetime there was genuine sporting apartheid in the Land of the Free.

Indeed, as late as 1961, Washington were still refusing to sign black players for no other reason than the owner didn't want to. Despite the clear superiority of integrated teams, they would have continued to do so – in the nation's capital – had their new stadium not been built on federal land, making them subject to employment discrimination legislation. The following season they became the last NFL team to integrate.

Somewhere between then and now, the NFL decided that not only was racism unacceptable, but it was something that needed to be tackled directly. In 2003, the Rooney Rule was brought in. It had two simple stipulations: when teams hire a new head coach, they must interview at least one ethnic minority candidate and they must document the process, providing written reasons for their final appointment. That's it, nothing else.

A curious symbol of sporting integrity.[15]

15 Sadly, the Rooney Rule is not named in honour of the then 17-year-old Wayne. It would've been lovely, would it not, if his amazing goal against David Seaman had been being replayed endlessly on ESPN as negotiations dragged on into the early hours and its startling, primeval beauty had reminded all the team owners that all of us – whatever our ethnic make-up – should be able to fall in love with the majesty of sporting excellence? Instead, rather more prosaically, it's named after Dan Rooney, Pittsburgh chairman and NFL blue blood.

It was a brilliant piece of legislation: simple to understand, simple to implement and creating no great administrative hardship for the people affected. Its impact was dramatic, though. Within three years the percentage of ethnic minority head coaches rose from six per cent to 22 per cent.

What NFL owners had admitted to themselves, rather bravely, was that, even though they were comfortable fielding teams where more than half their players were non-white, there was still lingering discrimination in coaching appointments. Like Dave Whelan after a flash of self-awareness, they recognised that there was an informal decision-making process at work that tended to preserve the status quo by short-listing people who the owners were comfortable with. People who were, well, *like* them (it's the same thing, presumably, that helps maintain the glass ceiling for women in business).

As Cyrus Mehri, one of the architects of the Rooney Rule, explained, the deceptively simple measure worked because it helped reform and professionalise the whole process of hiring head coaches. 'The Rooney Rule does not tell you who to hire. It just gets everybody to slow down… open their mind to a broad slate of candidates, including minority coaching candidates,' he says.

Crucially, he points out that it 'has also helped white coaching candidates who would have been overlooked. Rather than interview one candidate, teams interviewed ten.'[6] And, in interviewing ten as part of a documented hiring process that the league could audit, owners came to appreciate the merits of people who didn't fit the archetype of the head coach.

In other words, simple legislation like the Rooney Rule can tackle racism in sport not by forcing the hiring of black managers but by improving the quality of managerial appointments generally. All good candidates require, ethnic minority or otherwise, is equal consideration.

Compare with British football, whose persistent failure to address the subject rests on the unspoken argument that there's not *really* racism in managerial appointments, but even if there is, there's nothing we can do about it.

In early 2013 there was much fanfare from the PFA about adopting a version of the Rooney Rule in the UK. Disappointingly, though perhaps not unexpectedly, the so-called 'Coaching Fair Play' proposals were rejected by the Premier League. The Football League, meanwhile, agreed to give them consideration in the summer. The annual chairmen's meeting came and went in June, however, and no commitment or timetable for the proposals' implementation was agreed. Credit to the excellent work by campaigners in continuing to press the issue, but it really is quite remarkable – and shaming – that such a fight is still necessary.

It's been going on so long that it's hard to conclude that what this endless foot-dragging tells us is that, when the FA cracks down hard on on-field racism, it's not because it abhors it and is determined to drive it out of the game, but because it know the sponsors won't tolerate it. It doesn't fit with their brand values.

It forces us to face the ugly truth that the FA and Premier League do only what they have to to keep the game saleable. Such is the way of authorities who've abdicated their responsibility to provide leadership in favour of profit-maximising managerialism.

After 'Kick It Out', 'Show Racism The Red Card' and 'Financial Fair Play', football's pun generating machine gears up to spit out another in-no-way-insulting-to-your-intelligence initiative name.

The NFL has shown, meanwhile, that it has the lasting commitment necessary to make and to sustain change. At the end of the 2012/13 season, following several coaching changes, just four of 32 head coaches were from ethnic minorities (12.5 per cent), a drop from seven just two years earlier.

Rather than brush things under the carpet while the sponsors are looking the other way, the NFL is now considering if the Rooney Rule needs to be extended to the roles of offensive and defensive coordinator. These are the two most senior coaching roles beneath the head coach, and a key recruiting ground for future head coaches. As it was, 12 of the 62 offensive and defensive coordinators in the league were from ethnic minorities, accounting for 19 per cent of the total. This, the NFL thinks, isn't good enough.[16]

---

16 The NFL is far, of course, from being a paradise of egalitarian tolerance. Its attitude towards women, particularly, has come under a great deal of scrutiny. Not only does it still have cheerleaders – which is both incredibly prehistoric *and* probably the only part of the game that Richard Scudamore would approve of – but it's been dodging the issue of domestic violence for years. Or at least it was until Baltimore running back Ray Rice was caught on camera knocking out his girlfriend (now wife) in a casino lift in 2014 and then dragging her unconscious body part way out of the lift and into the corridor. In a disgraceful decision that nearly brought down the league commissioner, Rice was initially suspended for just two games. A slap on the wrist for a punch in the face, anti-domestic violence campaigners said. Later, though, when more footage emerged showing Rice delivering the blow, the NFL, claiming to have been misled by Rice about the events of the night, suspended him indefinitely, while his team, who'd previously backed him, fired him. There was a strong whiff here. Both Baltimore and the NFL appeared to have been going easy on domestic violence until the video tape made it impossible for them to do so. The league has since suspended a number of high-profile players for domestic violence and brought in stiff new penalties – as well as appointing advisors with a background in tackling domestic violence. They were bounced into tough action, though. How long it will take to change attitudes – attitudes like that of Rice's coach who described him as a 'heck of a guy' rather than 'a despicable human being' – is anyone's guess.

So, while the PFA is left dejectedly talking about how change can come from below, the NFL has made change right at the top and is now cascading it down.

One has to wonder why it should be so hard for football clubs to agree to *interview* one ethnic minority candidate. Not appoint them, just give them an interview. I can't be sure of their motives, but I rather doubt they're decent.

Racism, like John Terry's self-pity, is an ugly thing. Our failure to get angry about its persistence in football tells us much about ourselves but, above all, it tells us that football, without a lasting set of values to anchor it, is heading for the rocks.

It's a sport in the hands of individuals with such a conspicuous lack of moral purpose that it's no wonder so many of us are world-weary about the game. After all, these people who can't commit to making managerial hiring more diverse and meritocratic are the same folk charged with safeguarding the future of the most famous league in the world's most popular sport.

It is them who'll be entrusted with fighting off the destructive influence of the gambling syndicates. Them who'll have to tackle the twin problems of spiralling wages and club debts. Them who'll have to stop a future European Super League emasculating domestic football. Them who'll have to lead the fight to prevent the World Cup becoming a propaganda roadshow for hire, available to the highest bidder for North Korean-style displays of dictatorial prowess.

God help football.

8.

'I made a mistake. I accept full responsibility.'

Because they don't sack managers midway through the season.

YOU get into an empty lift. You're running late, so you hit the 'door close' button. But the doors don't close, at least not immediately. This half-second delay could cost you dearly so you press a second time, harder. Then, in rapid succession, a third, fourth and fifth time, before holding the button down until, finally, the doors close. There, you think, I sorted that out. Congratulations, you are ready to become the chairman of a football club.

Press and hold until someone who understands causation arrives.

Chairmen, like laboratory rats, astrology fans and people who regularly retweet urgent appeals, are hardwired to see themselves as important; to interpret themselves as an influential force in the universe. When a chairman sees a pretty girl in the street waving, he assumes it's at him. When he gets a ball of paper into the bin from across his office, he takes it as generally representative of his superior level of hand-eye coordination. And, when he fires a manager – the same man he appointed as the best candidate only a few years before – he is certain that he, and he alone, has saved his football club. Chairmen, like Steven Gerrard shaping for another Hollywood pass, just don't know when to stop.

But here's the thing: door close buttons in lifts were deactivated decades ago when it was realised that they hampered the optimum movement of people around a building (there's a reason trains wait at stations, even if there are no passengers to board). In many cases lifts still have them, but they don't work unless you have a key normally issued only to firefighters.[7] Pressing them has only one purpose: calming the passengers by making them feel more in control.

It is this need to rescue oneself from feelings of uselessness that contribute to some arresting statistics about job security in football management.

Going into the 2013/14 season, the average time in-post for the 20 managers in the Premier League was 1.84 seasons. And if that sounds low, it's worth considering that when you exclude the manager with the longest tenure – Arsene Wenger, then entering his 18th season with Arsenal – the average came down to 1.05 of a season. Amazingly, 15 of 20 managers had one or fewer seasons in charge at their current club.

Managerial tenure (in seasons) entering the 2013/14 season[17]

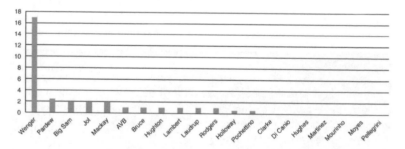

It's a remarkable statistic, but it's also misleading. Because something exceptional happened at the end of the 2012/13 season: seven of the eight longest serving managers in the Premier League retired (Ferguson), got a new job (Moyes and Martinez) or were sacked (Pulis, Mancini, McDermott and Adkins). At a stroke, virtually every manager in the Premier League with his feet under the table was on the move.

---

17 Seventy-five per cent of managers know where the toilet is but still have at least one player they refer to as 'big lad' because they haven't learnt everyone's name yet.

In fact, over the previous four years managerial tenure had held about steady. It was 3.67 seasons going into 2009/10, 3.53 seasons in 2010/11, 3.85 seasons in 2011/12 and 3.75 seasons in 2012/13. Suppose Ferguson had decided not to retire and had come back for the 2013/14 season (leaving Moyes at Everton). That decision alone would have changed the average from the headline 1.84 seasons to 3.74 seasons – in line with the broad trend.

So it's fair to say that job security doesn't seem to have got dramatically worse in recent years. Not only that, but Premier League tenure actually compares pretty well to the NFL. Over the last five years, the average time in-post of a Premier League manager is 3.33 seasons compared with 3.17 in the NFL.

Average tenure (in years) of manager/head coach at the start of each season

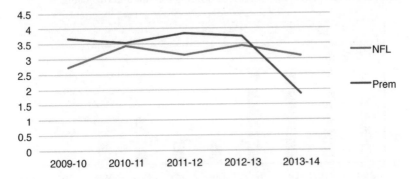

In other words – surprising and quite counter-intuitive words, granted – job security in the Premier League mightn't be getting that much worse. Others may maintain, and they may prove to be right, that Premier League tenure will continue to march downward and that, when Wenger is gone, we'll never again see any manager, no matter how successful, clock up ten or more years at a club.

What is certainly true, though, is that *when* and *why* you get sacked in the Premier League is different to the NFL. Which is where trigger happy chairmen come in.

In the NFL, team owners almost never sack someone except at the end of the year. Or if they do, it's usually after 13 or so of the 16 regular season games, when it's clear there's absolutely nothing left to play for.[18]

---

18 Here the NFL's separation of coaching and recruitment responsibilities also tends to help coaches see the season out. For all but a few teams, coaches contribute to but don't have the final say on drafting. This lies with the general manager. Unlike the January transfer window, which prompts chairmen to swing the axe to give the new guy time to recruit new players, there's little incentive to replace the coach since they don't even get involved in draft discussions with the scouting teams until after the season is over. There is, in other words, no head start to be had from firing your coach.

In 2013/14, eight of the 32 NFL teams – one in four – started the season with a new head coach. But not a single one had fired their previous coach until the 2012/13 season was over.

In fact, in the four seasons from 2009/10 to 2012/13, just seven head coaches were fired mid-season. And, crucially, only two were fired before their team had played ten games. In a 16-game season, this is equivalent to a Premier League manager being fired sometime before mid-January. Two of the other dismissals came after 11 games (mid-February by the Premier League calendar), while the final three were after 13 games (late March, say).

Sacking, then, is a tool very rarely used to try and improve a team's immediate performance in the NFL.[19] Instead it serves other time-dishonoured purposes like helping general managers defend their positions, bolstering season ticket sales with the promise of a new broom, putting players on notice and, of course, providing a sacrificial offering for fans and the media.

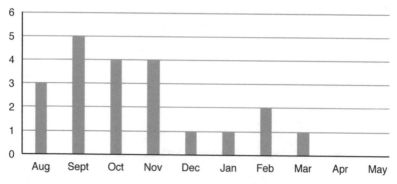

Month of first sacking in each Premier League season.[20]

If only Premier League owners had such restraint. In only four of the Premier League's first 21 seasons did the first sacking of the season come after the turn of the year. Roy McFarland went on 2 January in the 1995/96 season; Graeme Souness (2005/06) and Ian Porterfield (1992/93) lasted until February;

---

19 In 2014/15, Oakland tried reviving the idea of early sackings by firing their young head coach, Dennis Allen, just four games (all losses) into his third season. The last time a coach was fired that early was 2008, when Lane Kiffin was canned after winning just one of his first four games. Not by coincidence, Kiffin was also coaching in Oakland, a team that's become such a byword for underachievement that it makes Aston Villa look like a sporting dynasty. Kiffin's firing was also the last time that an NFL coach was dismissed with his team having played fewer than half of their fixtures. After Dennis Allen was sent packing, Oakland lost their next six games, finally winning against Kansas City to bring their record, as I write, to 1-10. No other team in the league has yet fired their coach.

20 A chairman's typical Saturday night: switch off new TV drama after five minutes. Call chauffeur to drive to restaurant. Get out and walk at end of drive. Leave restaurant after starter. Go to cinema. Leave during title sequence, discarding barely eaten popcorn. Get caretaker chauffeur to bring you home. Take credit for saving the evening.

and Danny Wilson was, amazingly, the first casualty of the 1999/00 season in March 2000.

Sackings in football, then, are not to clear the decks, but rather, like an atheist praying for a desperately sick relative, a frantic attempt to harness all forces of the universe to the cause of improving one's lot.

Panicking chairman, 'Dear Jesus, do me a solid this once and I promise never to give another vote of confidence to anyone.'

This is why, despite having a similar level of job security to an NFL head coach, as a Premier League manager you are *12 times* more likely to get sacked mid-season than a counterpart in the NFL.

So, while your average NFL team judges a coach's performance after three full seasons in charge, an English manager may end up being fired after just two and two half-seasons – a much less coherent body of work.

Not only does this demand results faster, but it also means that the first task of a newly appointed manager is likely to be firefighting, rather than planning, restructuring the backroom set-up or assessing the players. Hardly a good way to approach the complex business of remodelling a failing club. This is odd since club chairmen, like so many self-regarding mid-level business executives, are the kind of people who devour books like *The First 90 Days* and *The Seven Habits of Highly Effective People*, all the while nodding and thinking how many of the traits they recognise in themselves.

THINK

⚠

THEN ACT.

ALWAYS IN THAT ORDER.

Unless you are a football manager, in which case you must defy the iron law of business self-help books.

Leaving aside the sheer human cruelty of the whole sacking ritual – the agonising weeks of will-they-won't-they, the refusal to comment, the vote of confidence, the damaging leaks, the pretence of mutual agreement – the really terrible thing is that it's not clear that mid-season sackings actually work. Yes, sometimes a club that sacks its manager avoids relegation or makes a late dash for Europe – just as a club sometimes backs the manager of a struggling team and sees an improvement in results. But that doesn't prove it was the chairman's actions that made the difference.

Football is a world prone to magical as well as wishful thinking. Fans, players, managers and chairmen alike don't merely daydream of success, they engage in all kinds of superstitious activity to try and achieve it. For three-quarters of a season in the mid-90s, my friends and I – always the same four people in the same person's car – drove the same route to the ground and listened to the same four songs by the Smashing Pumpkins before turning the cassette tape off at the same roundabout. Until, that is, Billy Corgan's music stopped working and the goals dried up. Rather than concluding that the routine didn't and had never worked, we decided a new routine was required.

Team performances fluctuate over time so, if enough chairmen sack enough managers, a number of teams will experience seemingly miraculous escapes from relegation. In 2004/05 West Brom replaced Gary Megson in mid-season with Bryan Robson. Often cited as one of the greatest escapes in the history of football, West Brom won on the last day of the campaign to become the first club in Premier League history to be bottom at Christmas and still avoid relegation. Presumably the chairman felt pretty smug about that. After all, it takes a big and brave man to make a tough call when the chips are down. He virtually saved them himself.

Except that, the following year, West Brom were relegated with fewer points than the season Robson split with Megson. So did Robson really save them the previous year? And what would've happened had they stuck with Megson? Did firing him accomplish anything more than saddling West Brom with the cost of an extra salary? And anyway, which idiot was it who appointed Gary Megson *and* Bryan Robson?

The board of West Brom prepare to make some strategic changes to the running of the club.

The most comprehensive review of research into the impact of managers on results and managerial sackings is a report by Bell, Brooks and Markham published in 2013[8]. It covers research that showed that while sacking a manager does lead to a temporary improvement in results, clubs in similar situations who didn't sack their manager were more likely to see a sustained improvement in results. It quotes one study saying sacking a manager seems to be 'neither effective nor efficient in terms of improving team performance'. Another piece of research in the report looked at over 700 mid-season sackings in the UK from the early 1970s to the turn of the millennium before concluding simply, 'Clubs changing managers within season subsequently tended to perform worse than those that did not.'

So there are lots of reasons not to sack managers mid-season: it's not fair to sacked managers, it wastes a new manager's crucial first few months in charge, and, above all, it doesn't tend to improve club results.[21]

Despite the evidence suggesting that sacking, like Joey Barton, is a blunt tool, chairmen, like Jason McAteer at school, seem never to learn.

---

21 To be clear, I don't advocate never sacking a manager early in his tenure, provided a chairman ends the press conference by saying, 'I see now that I made a mistake in hiring David Moyes and, if it ever happens again that we so drastically misjudge an appointment, I will step down too.'

Most likely it's because of the asymmetry in decision-making. Fire a manager and if things improve you can take the credit. But back a manager who later takes you down and you'll be pilloried as gutless and gun-shy. Even if you fire a manager and still get relegated, you can say 'at least I tried to turn things around'.

Given all this, the hardest thing in the world is to stand by a manager – to stand by your own earlier judgment – and, at the end of the season, say, 'I believe you need to give a manager time to implement his plan. My judgment that he was the right person for the job was wrong and I made a mistake. I accept full responsibility.'

And that's why it's impossible to break the culture of firing managers mid-season. Like the rest of us, chairmen are weak, illogical, easily influenced people, unable to ignore a baying crowd. Like the rest of us, too often they don't bother to look at the evidence – or ignore it believing that they can beat the odds. Like the rest of us, chairmen think they're smarter, funnier and have better taste than average. They cross their fingers, read horoscopes and buy lottery tickets. And, like the rest of us would if we were ever put in that situation, chairmen find it easier to sack another human being than acknowledge their own mistakes.

Because chairmen, like Peter Beardsley in a house of mirrors, bring us face-to-face with the worst in ourselves. They remind us how craven, disloyal and foolish we can be when faced with criticism.

So hate your chairmen all you want, but recognise that there's no point expecting change. The odd great chairman who makes considered appointments and even more considered dismissals will never influence others. You either have character or you don't. The rest of us need the decision taking out of our hands.

In the NFL, as there's no relegation, there's much less incentive to make panic firings. Clearly, relegation is part of the lifeblood of football; the necessary winter to promotion's glorious summer. So what, then? Qualifications and courses for chairmen? We still haven't got past demanding managers be properly qualified for the job, so that's not going to fly (see chapter three).

That pretty much leaves one avenue: restricting the right of clubs to change managers during the season. A managerial transfer window, open only between May and August.

I know, I know. But if we want the game run better, with managerial appointments looking more like evidence-based decisions than childish tantrums, then we have to recognise that, at the bottom, we are all still idiots in lifts, vainly pressing buttons in the hope of getting somewhere a few seconds quicker.

9.

'I make my own decisions and I can hope for better.'

Because there are no feeder clubs.

IN 2011, in a disused warehouse in Walsall, the Premier League put a gun to the head of the Football League. 'We want the merchandise,' growled Richard Scudamore, the Premier League's fixer, 'and we're only going to pay you 20 per cent.'

'No,' wailed Greg Clarke, a senior Football League invertebrate, 'we can't live on that little.'

'Say yes or I'll put a £5m hole in you,' snarled Scudamore.

'Yes,' whimpered Clarke, soiling himself. 'Thank you, master.'

'Right,' Scudamore barked to his goons, 'round up the kids and let's get out of here.'[22]

Richard $cudamore: a shiny-faced, former-Yellow Pages salesman.

---

22 I should like to make it clear, for the benefit of Mr Scudamore's lawyers, that the above did not literally happen. I probably shouldn't have to say that it's a joke, a satirical flight of fancy. But then, having seen the jokes Richard Scudamore shares with his friends, one can never tell what some people will find funny.

The market for young players is a microcosm of the collapse of British social bonds. The rich and powerful openly exploit the weak, accumulating an ever more disproportionate share of the spoils, all the while claiming they're just playing by the rules of the game. Meanwhile, their hired hands are at work rewriting the rules to further unbalance the game. If challenged, they will modestly proclaim themselves nothing more than the winners in a winner-takes-all society.

These days, you might think that the wealthy are running short of things to complain about. Sadly not. Especially in football, where a sense of entitlement metastasises inside the game, hollowing-out players, agents, executives and administrators into ghastly amoral husks.

Unnamed Premier League player giving thanks to Richard Scudamore.

Depending on how Theo Walcott, Gareth Bale and Alex Oxlade-Chamberlain perform, Southampton will earn between £22m and £37m from their sale. Even for a club of their size, that's decent money considering none had played a single game in the Premier League when they left the Saints. Imagine, though, if Southampton had had the financial security to hold on to them. That would be an interesting young Premier League midfield, especially if they'd stayed long enough to be joined by Luke Shaw and Adam Lallana.

Even when you get a reasonable price for your stars, there's still something that rankles about the inevitability of any emerging talent being hoovered up by Premier League clubs exploiting the financial imbalance in the game. We cherish our homegrown players; they stockpile them like venture capitalists backing cash-poor young businesses. We want these young people to succeed;

they care only that a certain percentage of their investments blow up, Gareth Bale-style, and give them a huge return.

This kind of financial, organisational or physical coercion occurs anywhere where one party holds power over another. For decades, the tribunal system mitigated it by making sure smaller clubs didn't get too terrible a deal. It was as if a school employed a bullying monitor to intervene in playground thefts and return to the victim just enough of their lunch money to buy a packet of crisps.

'I'm going to give you three nuggies and a dead-arm for 90 per cent of your packed lunch.'

Eventually, though, even this wasn't enough for the Premier League. In 2011, under the guise of improving the England team, Football League clubs were strong-armed into accepting the Elite Professional Performance Plan (EPPP). Premier League clubs got all their Christmases at once, with a big increase in time they could spend with their academy players and an abolition of the rule that limited recruitment to those living within 90 minutes of the club. The former may leave youth-teamers, most of whom will never become established professionals, even more poorly equipped for life outside football. The latter will undermine the ability of non-Premier League academies to recruit talent from their local area.

But the real killer was the new tariff for valuing young players who move between academies. From now on, academy players will have a fixed fee based on their years at the club, the status of its academy and the number of appearance they make for their new club.

According to *The Guardian*, in 2009, when Everton signed Luke Garbutt, then 16 years old, from Leeds United, the tribunal fee was 'an initial £600,000. Under the new system this would have been capped at a maximum of £131,000.'[9]

Previously, to avoid a tribunal, clubs had to offer an amount based on their estimated future valuation of a player, discounted by the uncertainty of talent translating into success. Now, with the majority of the money paid becoming performance-related, the investment has been hugely de-risked for the Premier League.

Tottenham had to pay Palace £700,000 at tribunal for John Bostock, with significant add-ons and a sell-on clause. This seemed a reasonable balance of risk and reward for someone with great talent but no track record. Under the new scheme, with Bostock given a free transfer this summer having never made a league appearance at Spurs, Palace's compensation would've been well south of £100,000. Barely enough to keep Simon Jordan orange for a year. While Bostock didn't make it for Spurs, Palace could very well have done with him the last few years.

Henry Scudamore: once sued by his wife for being impotent. Best known for having commissioned the world's most expensive cabinet.[23]

Southampton are one of the few clubs whose academy received the highest rating under the EPPP's grading system while outside of the Premier League. Depending on the rating, the amount of compensation you receive per player varies from £12,500–£40,000 per year of coaching given.

Suppose Southampton find a nine-year-old they think is the new Gareth Bale. And suppose he stays until he's 16 (the maximum period you can be compensated for), before being whisked away to a Premier League club, where he plays 100 times for them (the maximum number of appearances for which you can be compensated). In this scenario, the most Southampton could get would be £1.5m.

---

23 Look up the 'Badminton Cabinet'. It's not some dubious public school punishment. It's much worse than that.

So, in future, no Premier League team will ever have to pay more for a youngster – no matter how extraordinary they turn out to be – than the base fee that Chelsea are supposed to have paid MK Dons for 14-year-old Seyi Ojo just two years ago. According to the BBC, under the new scheme, he would've cost Chelsea less than £150,000. And even then that comes with a DFS-style payment plan: since it could take years for the player to break into the first team and make those 100 appearances, the money will be paid in dribs-and-drabs, with no big lump sum to ease a smaller club's cash-flow problems.[10]

Oh, yes, and sell-on clauses have gone as well.

In the future, then, Premier League clubs will simply take the best talent from the lower divisions knowing that, if they succeed, the costs are capped and, if they don't, the players can be discarded, almost cost-free. It's like mugging someone to buy lottery tickets on the promise of sharing some of the winnings.

As with the dominant players in most industries, the Premier League's professed commitment to competition and the free market is a cover for a helpless addiction to regulation and intervention. They *love* regulation – provided they are the ones doing the regulating. So overtaken by greed is the Premier League that there's seemingly no thought to morality, fairness or the broader needs of the game. Once this happens, any money-making opportunity not actually illegal becomes inevitable and then, in short order, compulsory.

If you're in any doubt as to what kind of a deal EPPP was for the Football League, you need only to know that, to get it through, the Premier League threatened to withdraw £5.4m in so-called solidarity payments if the League didn't agree. Even then, only 60 per cent of League clubs voted in favour.

'Don't mess with Scudamore, he's one tough paisan.'

Increasingly, then, the new economics of player valuation will incentivise Premier League clubs to strip academies of young players before they can even make their first-team debuts, let alone reach an age where a seven-figure transfer fee might be necessary. I'm mostly concerned here with fairness and what this tells us about the balance of power in the game; I'll leave you to decide what the likely impact of concentrating talent in a smaller number of academies will be. Higher quality academy graduates and more young British players in the Premier League? Or more careers stifled from a lack of first-team opportunities?

Historically, football has always celebrated its smaller clubs. It was a community of 92 clubs, equal in dignity if not size. Change was slow but it *was* possible and, if you supported your team for long enough, you would be rewarded with the odd promotion – maybe even to the First Division. There was no shame in having a run-down stadium and, before the FA Cup became a schedule-clogging inconvenience, you'd have a shot at national acclaim if you could pull off a giant-killing.

James Scudamore: Royalist MP who left the country rather than pay his gambling debts.

But, gradually, as in politics, business and media, the wealthy have sought to entrench their dominance. We don't celebrate the underdog quite as we did. Instead poverty and low social standing have been stigmatised and redefined as personal failure. And, rather than being content with organic growth, many fans greet an offer to buy their club – with money expropriated from the poor of other nations – not with caution, but as a chance 'to take the club to the next level'. The city gates are thrown open and the Mongol hordes welcomed.

And why? Because nowadays the Premier League *is* English football.

The game now centres on the needs of a group of ten to 15 clubs, nouveau riche social climbers trying to pretend they don't have an embarrassing extended family of variable means and questionable table manners.

The Premier League isn't interested in international football. And it would rather do without relegation. In fact, it would probably quite happily see every League club in the country shut down to maximise TV audiences for its product. So while feeder clubs are technically banned in British football, there's no mistaking the Football League's last remaining value to the Premier League: as a place for its young players to get experience.[24]

But only on loan, you understand; valuable commodities must never again be owed by Football League clubs. In future, all non-Premier League players will become simply footballing pacemakers, members of an extended network of Premier League practice squads designed to prepare young stars for being fouled by Marouane Fellaini.

It's always been tough at the bottom, of course. Cash-flow problems, low attendances, the difficulties of finding and retaining good players and managers. But, among the grassless pitches and decaying stands, there was some honour and respect to be found.[25]

One doesn't have to romanticise footballing poverty to recognise that not everyone can be in the Premier League and have 40,000-plus fans each week. For the health of the game, it's critical that football at every level is valued in its own right and its meaning to its communities celebrated.

In 2004, Professor Sir Michael Marmot, a British epidemiologist, published 'Status Syndrome', in which he looked at the impact on people's health of having a sense of control over their lives, having a sense of self-worth and earning the esteem of peers. What he discovered was extraordinary: respect and esteem are so valuable to our health that they have a measurable impact on life expectancy. He found that, controlling for other factors, winning an Oscar added *four years* to the life of an actor compared with that of actors who were nominated for, but didn't win, an Oscar. Four extra years for being a winner, instead of a runner-up.[11]

---

24 Feeder clubs proper have, of course, been pushed recently. The source of the initiative was, puzzlingly, not the Premier League, whose self-interest would need no explanation, but Greg Dyke. And that doesn't make a whole lot of sense unless, when you watched the World Cup, your first thought was, 'The England team's lack of experience in the Johnstone's Paint Trophy is painfully apparent.' One might even go further and say that, by opposing Sepp Blatter and his asset strippers but proposing B teams for the Premier League, the FA shows that it objects only to the rich having to actually grease palms to get what they want.

25 In chapter five I criticised football's reluctance to embrace statistics, but, in truth, fans of small clubs understand 'regression to the mean' only too well. This gentle pessimism of the experienced loser is why we don't get carried away when our team is on the verge of historic success.

Ferguson, 'You're on borrowed time, pal.' Wenger, 'Just wait till Abou Diaby comes back for us.'

It might sound frivolous but it set Marmot off combing through the health records of British civil servants – a huge and carefully stratified dataset. He found that there is strong correlation between good health and seniority. The better paid, more powerful, more highly acclaimed you are, the longer you live. Far from the popular image of the stressed CEO dropping dead of overwork, you're much more likely to suffer a heart attack if you are near the bottom of the ladder.

At this point I'd like to invite Professor Marmot to do a study looking at the average life expectancy of Stockport fans compared to those of Manchesters United and City to see if supporting a perpetually unsuccessful team sends people to an early grave.

If the struggle for respect is so important a part of our lives, what will be the impact on lower-division football of the continuing dominance of the Premier League?

Fans don't expect player loyalty. They know the days of single-club players are over. There is, though, something totemic about the ability to develop and keep good players and managers. When a star elects to sign a new contract rather than move on, the message from the club to the world is, 'I may not be a winner, but I am in charge of my own destiny. I make my own decisions and I can hope for better.' Conversely, few reminders of one's smallness are as sobering as when a big club announces to the press that they are considering buying one of your stars. Because, if you can't even hold on to your one good player, what chance have you ever got of building a team? You are left feeling as impotent as Pelé, as worthless as an agent, as useless as Nigel Winterburn on his right foot.

Richard Scudamore unveils the Premier League's blueprint for the future of football.

In the NFL, it's a basic precept of administering the game that for the league to succeed all clubs have to grow. Instead of competing against each other for a bigger slice of the pie, the collective aim is to bake a bigger pie.

This might sound puzzling coming from a country that celebrates personal wealth and excess like no other. But, for some reason, American football has never viewed success as a zero-sum game. It believes that all teams contribute equally to a worthwhile competition – even those who lose – and that, for any team to progress, it must find and develop its own players, not cherry-pick another's. The NFL, then, is a curious enclave of benevolent corporatism in a land of catastrophic vulture capitalism.

As a result, assuming it's well run and managed, every team, no matter how bad its current group of players, can legitimately dream of winning a Super Bowl within five years. How many teams can dream of reaching the summit of the Premier League in that timescale without a new and very rich owner?

Presently in the lower divisions, if you have a great young talent, enjoy them while you can. The moment you have one building block of your team in place, it gets snatched away, like a Lego piece in a toddlers' tower-building contest. What you need, then, is a gradual accumulation of players. Rather than find someone brilliant, you want to keep upgrading a bit at a time, making sure never to attract attention by having anyone outstanding.

In contrast, the NFL is set up to prevent a group of elite teams becoming dominant by feeding off small clubs. There can be no Big Four.

The whole way players are acquired, retained and paid is underpinned by structures – like the draft and the salary cap – which are designed to keep the league competitive. Indeed, there is a system of player contracts specifically

Edwyn Scudamore-Stanhope: aged 46, the King's 'Master of the Horse' married a 21-year-old. Pervert.

created to make sure that every team can hold on to its very best players. Chief among these are restricted free agency and the franchise tag.

'Restricted free agency' applies to a player who is out of contract and hasn't yet played three seasons where he's appeared in six or more of his team's 16 games. In this situation, while an emerging young player can negotiate with other teams, his current team have the right to retain him by matching the offer of any other team (bear in mind that, with the salary cap, no team can entice away another's player by simply offering to triple their wages – unless they balance it with salary cuts elsewhere. Unlike the Premier League, now suffering Weimar Republic levels of hyperinflation, an NFL full-back's wages don't need to be delivered in a wheelbarrow).

The 'franchise tag', meanwhile, allows each team to nominate one player a season, with whom they've not been able to agree a contract, as someone they want to keep. In return for paying him a 20 per cent increase or the league average of the top five best paid players in his position (whichever is the greater), he must then play for them.

What this means is that, if a player becomes a star and then decides he wants to get more money, clubs can buy themselves time to find and develop replacements. Since all teams face the restrictions of a salary cap, the effect tends to be that clubs only let players become free agents if they are unwilling – rather than unable – to match their salary demands. Typically, then, only mid- and lower-rank talents become free agents.

As in football, players under contract can request a trade. But, unlike football, NFL transfer fees aren't paid in cash. They come in draft picks, of which each team has a very limited number each year. This acts as a kind of 'transfer cap', preventing rich teams making offers that can't be refused.

The result of all this is that smaller NFL teams can build squads piece by piece and, provided they manage their salary cap prudently, they can do so without fear of being bullied into surrendering their best talent. As a consequence, it's not uncommon, even now, for all-time greats to be one-club players. Most clubs have had, and held on to, a Steve Bull or Matthew Le Tissier-like legend in the last decade.

I don't say any of this believing that the franchise tag could be introduced to football or, even if it were, that it would necessarily transform the game – well, certainly not like a salary cap would. That's not the purpose of this or any other of the essays in this book; I don't think for a second that all football's problems can be solved by simply adopting NFL ideas.

What I do think, though, is that the NFL provides an illuminating comparison; a framework for identifying and enumerating the many ills of football. It helps show just how much is wrong with the game and, crucially, how much comes down to one central problem: the lack of disinterested, collectively minded administration of our national sport.

Football, plainly speaking, is in the hands of wolves. Not Mick McCarthy-bred tame, toothless, long-ball relegation fodder, but a pack of frenzied, insatiable animals, gorging themselves on the game, unable and unwilling to stop, even if it means killing it.

The NFL, which has more than its share of greedy egomaniacs in every boardroom and locker-room, shows that, if a sport is run properly, it can be hugely popular and massively profitable – and still provide every team with a chance to compete and every fan with a dream of success.

In other words, if America's national sport can preserve something of the Corinthian spirit, then football isn't lost. Yet.

10.

'I can see the pub from here!'
Because you can drink during the game.

IS there anything more wonderful than grainy footage of Diego Armando Maradona on the charge, barrelling past defenders like a ballet-dancing bull? Is there anything more awe-inspiring than Wenger's Invincibles on the quick break, otherworldly in their spindle-shanked, lockstep precision? Is there anything better able to unite disparate peoples in hope and optimism than a hard-fought World Cup giant-killing? In short, is there anything that brings more joy and happiness to mankind than football?

In fact, there is. It's called beer and they sell it during American football games.

I was once in a riot; a pretty ugly one. I'll come back to it later, but I mention it now because I remember the bad old days of football violence and I

Beer: tastes really nice.

understand the part alcohol played in it. We mustn't let it obscure one simple point, however: sport is better when you can enjoy it with friends and a beer.

Beer is, as we know, a social and mental lubricant, apt – in the right quantities – to make one more outgoing and more expansive in one's thinking. This makes it a valuable part of sporting enjoyment, analysis and contemplation. And yet, sadly, in the UK its consumption is prohibited during the actual event. As a result, the act of watching sport and analysing it are separate activities, with the latter performed in pubs and on sofas, removed physically and temporally from the event under discussion.

Beer: helps you unpick strategies and recognise illuminating historical comparisons.

Beer – like psychoactive drugs for music – makes great football better and bad football tolerable. Which is handy because, unless your team is on its once-in-a-decade upswing, most league fixtures tend to be pretty poor.

Yes, you can buy beer at grounds, but the effect is muted if you can only drink it in the concourse. There's a reason people have house parties instead of multi-storey car park parties.

The half-time beer is especially disappointing. The whistle blows, you rush to the bar, queue for ten minutes and then have to down your pint immediately, lest you miss a goal. Encouraging punters to drink like alcoholics at last orders is not, I suggest, a good way to create a more convivial atmosphere at sporting events. The last time I was at Wembley for an England match, there were three food options: burger and chips, fish and chips and chicken and chips. Not an ideal menu for a vegetarian. With my £5 carrier bag of Minstrels – the smallest size available – I chugged a beer that had been pre-poured and then slowly brought up to room temperature. Watching England play is stomach-churning enough without that combination inside you.

Ayresome Park: scene of the most expensive beer I ever bought.[26]

In the same year, I went to Wembley to watch Minnesota play Pittsburgh in one of the annual NFL games. This time the range of food was much wider – there were pizza, nachos and numerous other melted-cheese-delivery systems available. And, quite delightfully, not only was beer served until about half an hour from the end, it was even permitted in the seated area. How civilised.

Beer: more portable than the authorities would have you believe.

---

26 I once drove five hours to Middlesbrough, ducked out after 44 minutes to go and queue for beer, missed the only goal in an utterly terrible away defeat, and then had to drive five hours home.

And this is one of the reasons that the NFL is a more enjoyable experience than the Premier League. With longer games and more scoring (so nipping out to the toilet need not wait until half-time), you can relax, drink and chew the fat – as well as the food.

Before old-style tin shack stadiums were demolished and clubs moved to out-of-town facilities, there was always a pub nearby where you could dine unhurriedly with friends on a nourishing pre-match meal of beer and crisps. Now, with many modern stadiums lacking any hinterland, the game-day experience has been compressed into a two-and-a-half-hour window that begins with paying £10 to park on an industrial estate and ends with being shepherded rapidly from the ground at the final whistle. It's a social experience on a par with cinema: close proximity to many but no actual enjoyment of each other's company.[27]

American sport took the problem of out-of-town stadiums and made it an opportunity. Over there, people arrive early and 'tailgate': they barbecue, drink, talk and play games in the car park before going into the stadium. It's like a giant car boot sale, except that, instead of selling junk, there are thousands of people grilling sausages and drinking beer. People of Britain – as with New York and the internet and *The Wire* and enormous slices of pizza – sometimes you just have to stand back and applaud and say, 'America, you are awesome!'

Tailgating is an experience designed to make you feel like a welcome guest. Quite a contrast to football where fans are regarded as little more than an inconvenience that the club, stewards and police tolerate only because someone has to pay the bills.

The NFL, then, is sport as it should be: social, convivial and with fans treated as adults.

Serving alcohol during games is not without problems, of course. Drunkenness can be an issue, especially in needle matches, but it doesn't come close to the threat levels found in a typical British town centre on a Saturday night, let alone a football ground from decades gone by. The reasons are many and complex, but it's notable that, with some NFL teams allowing their fans to begin tailgating up to five hours before the game, there was an average of just 27 ejections and three arrests per game last season.[12] This compares favourably with the abstemious Premier League, where there were 2.14 arrests per match in 2012/13.[13]

So, back to the riot. It was the early 1990s, in a run-down stadium I still called home until quite recently. Swansea were visiting which, back then, was a grudge match for virtually every team in the division, so aggressive and unpleasant were their players and fans alike.

Before the game there was talk on the terraces that groups of the Swansea faithful had been turning over cars and smashing windows in the town centre. Whatever the truth, there was something evil in the air.

From the beginning, a fractious game was interrupted by pitch invasions. Egged on by a Swansea player, the supporters grew ever more raucous. Some

---

27 You can see a video recreation of the typical walking distance between a modern
    football stadium and nearest licensed venue by YouTubing the phrase 'I can see
    the pub from here.'

climbed the floodlights while others began throwing objects into the home end. Then, apparently in retaliation for a policeman coshing a pitch invader, about a third of the travelling fans tore down fencing and kicked over the pitchside brick wall, using the debris to attack the police and home fans. A full-scale riot ensued. Not a little pushing and shoving, I should emphasise, but bricks, glass and planks used as weapons with intent against riot shields, Alsatians and police horses.

It was an experience uglier than watching an Alex McLeish-coached team of champion gurners playing one-touch on a bumpy pitch.

Visiting a football game these day makes all this seem like a lifetime ago. The atmosphere, location and demographics of football have changed and I'm not convinced that allowing people to sit and chat over a beer during the game would bring about the return of violent disorder in the stands. For one thing, people drink slower when sitting down.[14]

Beer: effective and capable of being administered safely.

I doubt I'll ever have a chance to be proved wrong, though. In Britain we've allowed ourselves to be convinced that we can't be trusted.

So, instead, I'll think of you all when I'm next at Wembley, an honorary American for the day.

11.

'I didn't want to be in a league where I can't compete on management.'

Because they have the draft.

I N hindsight, the summer of 2004 came to be seen as the moment when the whole balance of power changed in the Premier League. For it was then that Glenn Hoddle laid the groundwork for the Wolves team that would dominate domestic and European football for a decade by signing two immensely promising youngsters: Wayne Rooney and Robin van Persie.

It's hard to believe now, given his acclaim as the greatest manager of his generation, but things hadn't started well for Hoddle. Taking over a forlorn team in early December 2003, he was unable to extricate Wolves from the relegation zone and they finished bottom. Not by much though. On equal points and equal goal difference, their last-place finish and subsequent first

'God wants me to say something stupid and lose my job.'

pick in the following draft rested on having scored just two fewer goals than 19th-placed Leeds. On such fine margins are sporting futures made and broken.

In the draft, Hoddle selected the obvious choice: 17-year-old prodigy Wayne Rooney. Elsewhere in a strong year, Arjen Robben went to perennial strugglers Manchester City, while a then-unknown Xabi Alonso joined Blackburn, creating – with Tugay – the Premier League's craftiest midfield pairing.

The real steal of the draft wasn't in the first round, though. With the 21st pick, Hoddle showed his genius, taking a player that every other club had passed on, owing to his suspect temperament: 20-year-old Dutchman Robin van Persie. At a stroke, the greatest forward line in English football since Rush and Dalglish was formed. Wolves won the Championship at a canter before establishing themselves as one of the most feared attacking forces in the Premier League.

Leeds, meanwhile, used their first-round pick on Paulo Ferreira and their second on Thimothée Atouba, blowing their relegation parachute totally and condemning themselves to lower-division football for many years to come.

Eight years ago, somewhere else in the multiverse, Rooney and van Persie first came together at The Enchantment Under the Sea Dance.[28]

Dynasties are something we've grown sadly used to in the Premier League, with wealth and squad strength the twin elements of a feedback loop driving an ever greater concentration of income and resources at the top clubs.

How different it could've all been if English football had had the draft – one of the NFL's Holy Trinity of mechanisms designed to promote equality (the salary cap and equal TV revenue sharing being the other two).

The way it works is simple. Teams take turns picking in reverse order, with the worst team getting the first choice of the young players joining the league. Once all 32 teams have picked a player, they start again and continue, round after round, until the new talent is allocated.

It's a system designed to ensure that only quality of management, rather than wealth, engenders and perpetuates success or failure.

---

28   They danced to the sound of Michael J. Fox playing 'Jonny Evans B. Goode'.

To British ears, it sound radical and utterly unthinkable – basically communism with fireworks, cheerleaders and shoulder pads. Until, that is, you remind yourself that it's a ritual performed daily in every playground in the country as a way of getting balanced teams. If even seven-year-olds understand the importance of competition, it makes you wonder why adults tolerate such a damagingly unfair market for football players.

Children picking teams.[29]

To show how different things could be with a draft, imagine you took the most expensive players bought each year by Premier League clubs (for the purposes of this thought-experiment, we'll include only players aged 25 and under, since few players graduate and join the NFL later than that). Then, instead of distributing the players to the teams with the most money, we'll parcel them out in reverse order, according to the previous season's final league table.

This would mean that, in 2005/06, Michael Essien would have joined relegated Norwich, while Nemanja Vidic would have provided some steel not to Manchester United's defence but Birmingham's. Theo Walcott, meanwhile, would've brought his deceptively purposeless pace to Charlton's last season in the Premier League. The following year, Gareth Bale would've been making heart shapes not at White Hart Lane but at overweight, shirtless Geordie men instead. And, in later seasons, we would've seen Modric bringing much needed

---

29 Jose, 'I'll take Tommy.'
      Roberto, 'And I'll take Adam.'
      Jose, 'Actually, I want Adam. I'll give you a 50p mix for him.'
      Roberto, 'Ok...John.'
      Jose, 'Oh, yeah, and I want John as well. You can have Kelvin, Bryan or Sam.'
      Roberto, 'Kelvin's in detention, Sam's blind in one eye and Bryan wore his wellies to school today.'
      Jose, 'Ready to play? Team that wins gets first pick tomorrow...'

guile to Sunderland, Mascherano carrying water in the Reading midfield and Robinho fitfully delighting the Derby faithful after their relegation.

To bring us a bit more up to date, have a look what it would've meant in 2012/13 and 2013/14 – and see who your team would've picked. Yes, it would've been a different league indeed.

Round 1				Round 2		
Pick	Club	Player		Pick	Club	Player
1	Wolves	Eden Hazard		21	Wolves	Christian Benteke
2	Blackburn	Oscar		22	Blackburn	César Azpilicueta
3	Bolton	Javi Garcia		23	Bolton	Jay Rodriguez
4	QPR	Mousa Dembélé		24	QPR	Vurnon Anita
5	Villa	Joe Allen		25	Villa	Marko Marin
6	Wigan	Shinji Kagawa		26	Wigan	Esteban Granero
7	Stoke	Matija Nastasic		27	Stoke	Mapou Yanga-Mbiwa
8	Sunderland	Steven Fletcher		28	Sunderland	Scott Sinclair
9	Norwich	Gastón Ramírez		29	Norwich	Kevin Mirallas
10	Swansea	Daniel Sturridge		30	Swansea	Nick Powell
11	West Brom	Jack Rodwell		31	West Brom	Sung-Yong Ki
12	Fulham	Fabio Borini		32	Fulham	Modibo Maiga
13	Liverpool	Hugo Lloris		33	Liverpool	Alexander Buttner
14	Everton	Adam Johnson		34	Everton	Steven Nzonzi
15	Chelsea	Jan Vertonghen		35	Chelsea	Matthew Lotwon
16	Newcastle	Olivier Giroud		36	Newcastle	Oussama Assaidi
17	Tottenham	Wilfried Zaha		37	Tottenham	Robert Snodgrass
18	Arsenal	Victor Moses		38	Arsenal	Chris Gunter
19	Man City	Coutinho		39	Man City	Adrian Mariappa
20	Man Utd	Gylfi Sigurðsson		40	Man Utd	Joe Bennett

The 2012/13 Premier League draft.[30]

Just looking at the 2012/13 draft, and based on how we know those players have developed, you can already see how that season's Premier League might've been a far more intriguing proposition.

According to Canada's National Endowment for Financial Education, 70 per cent of people who unexpectedly come into large sums of money will lose it within seven years.[15] In Tottenham's case, it took barely seven hours. Like the Harrods delivery van arriving at Elton John's house, until the wrapping paper is off, we won't know for a while exactly what's been bought and what will prove worth keeping from that year's transfer window splurge. The suspicion, however, must be that Tottenham swapped a once-in-a-generation talent for Christian Eriksen and a handful of magic beans.

---

30 Methodology: Take the most expensive players under 25 who joined a Premier League club in that season. Group into blocks of 20 (for the number of clubs) and then allocate in reverse order according to the final standings from previous season's league table. Academy players, like Jack Wilshere, have been excluded as it would've necessitated placing a figure on their perceived value when they graduated to the first team. Fee data from Transfermarket.co.uk.

Round 1		
Pick	Club	Player
1	QPR	Mesut Özil
2	Reading	Willian
3	Wigan	Marouane Fellaini
4	Sunderland	Érik Lamela
5	Newcastle	Steven Jovetic
6	Wigan	André Schürrle
7	Southampton	Paulinho
8	Stoke	Mamadou Sakho
9	Fulham	Andy Carroll
10	Norwich	James McCarthy
11	West Ham	Victor Wanyama
12	Swansea	Wilfried Bony
13	West Brom	Christian Eriksen
14	Liverpool	Étienne Capoue
15	Everton	Simon Mignolet
16	Tottenham	Ricky van Wolfswinkel
17	Arsenal	Dejan Lovren
18	Chelsea	Jozy Altidore
19	Man City	Vlad Chiriches
20	Man Utd	Marco van Ginkel

Tints indicate from top to bottom: Relegated, Lower half, Top half, Qualified for Europe, Won title

The 2013/14 Premier League draft: the worst off-seasons signings ever?

Now, if you think it's unforgiving being the manager of a City, United, Chelsea or Arsenal, imagine if you were expected to deliver continued success without a huge transfer budget or the lion's share of young talent. Wenger and Ferguson often managed to supplement a few keys-signings with homegrown or lesser talents, but could they have done it without buying Bergkamp, Rooney, Ferdinand or Henry?

Five of Wenger's ten most expensive signings – Reyes, Wiltord, Arshavin, Jeffers and Hleb – rank somewhere between failures and total disasters. From Ferguson's top ten, the only outright wastes of money were Veron and Anderson. Berbatov and Nani would certainly count as disappointments, though. If that seems like quite a poor strike rate for big money signings, it's worth noting that, for many other large clubs, it's quicker just to list the players who were actually a success.

The free-for-all of the Premier League transfer market creates a situation where an extraordinary failure rate for signings is both inevitable and tolerated. It also provides a ready-made set of excuses for managers. Poor signings at a small club? It's all we could afford. Poor signings at a big club? No matter, two years from now, when the player can be judged a clear failure, he will have been replaced by another big-money signing, all the while his cost being eroded by continual inflation in transfer fees.

In the NFL, however, players who flop are far more noticeable and costly. The draft is immune to changes in buying power; a first-round pick is a first-round pick. If he fails – if the player you judged best available to you in a given year doesn't provide five or more seasons of good service – then there's no hiding place. He didn't just cost you what you paid him in wages; he cost you the performance of every other player you him picked in preference to.

Imagine now that you are Manuel Pellegrini taking over at Manchester City, with the Premier League about to introduce a draft for the first time. Your instructions from Sheikh Mansour, patient man that he is, are to regain the title or lose your job. But, instead of giving you a blank cheque to improve the squad, he gives you only the 19th, 38th, 57th, 76th, 95th, 114th and 133rd pick in the draft. Anyone else you want will have to be a free agent.

How then do you go about building a footballing dynasty? Well, for starters, you'd better be a brilliant coach and an astute tactician. And you'd better be able, year after year, to spot and develop talent that others will overlook.

Bill Belichick is the Alex Ferguson of the NFL. In 14 seasons as head coach of New England he's won three Super Bowls, lost two more and taken his team to the AFC Championship Game (effectively, the Super Bowl semi-final) three times. He's only failed to make the play-offs three times – and only once in the last ten years.

'You hear that, men? It's squeaky bum time.'

In Premier League terms, this would mean finishing in the top three in seven of the last 12 seasons. If that sounds slightly less magnificent than Ferguson's achievements, bear in mind that this is in a sport where, instead of a 38-game season, there are only 16 fixtures, followed by a knockout competition. These differences introduce a much higher element of randomness into the final standings in the NFL – making it far harder to keep a team at the top.

In addition, Belichick's continued success has meant that he's been picking, on average, 26th out of 32 teams in the draft. Other than when he's made trades, only once has his team had a top 20 pick. In any given year, in any given sport, only a handful of obviously great players appear. They rarely hang around until the 26th pick – unless, like a young van Persie, they're perceived to have temperament problems.

This is why, in the NFL, there's no such thing as a chequebook manager. You can trade picks for players – or to move higher in the draft to improve your chance of getting who you want – but even here, Belichick is at a disadvantage. Other things being equal, all teams have the same number of draft picks, which means the first-round pick of a perennially successful club is worth less than that of almost any other team, since you know it's likely to be a late pick when the real talent has gone.

Despite this, Belichick has wheeled and dealed, coached and upskilled, and managed to produce sustained success. To be the best manager in the NFL, then, means not just being the best motivator and tactician, it means constantly being able to do more with less than any other manager in the game. Belichick has delivered Big Four results on Bottom Three budgets. Tom Brady, for example, who's the greatest player of his generation and the quarterback around whom Belichick built his team, was drafted 199th in the sixth round of the 2000 draft.

And while Belichick has scowled around the top of the league for ten years, others have risen and fallen. Denver and Seattle – the two strongest teams in the NFL in 2013/14 – both experienced significant down periods recently. Denver didn't qualify for the play-offs between 2006 and 2010, while Seattle had four years, between 2008 and 2011, where they won fewer than half of their games. Meanwhile, 2012/13's beaten Super Bowl team, San Francisco, went eight years,

'You let the best team – the one that already has the best players – buy all the other good players?'

from 2003 to 2010, without a single season when they won more games than they lost – making them the seventh worst team of the decade.

As I write this chapter – a quarter of the way through the 2013 season – Pittsburgh and the New York Giants are two of only four teams who have lost all of their games. And yet these teams have won four Super Bowls – two each – in the last eight years.

One of the other two winless teams is Tampa Bay, who themselves won the Super Bowl as recently as 2003. In that game they beat Oakland – a team with three Super Bowl appearances and two victories – who started this season labelled as the worst squad in NFL history.

Sitting just above the winless teams, with a solitary victory, are Philadelphia, who won just four games in the whole of last season and who are rebuilding under a new management. Their previous coach took them to nine play-offs, including one Super Bowl appearance, between 2000 and 2010.

In fact, only three of 32 teams in the NFL – Oakland, Cleveland and Buffalo – haven't had a single play-off appearance in the last decade.

And that's why the draft is brilliant – and why Belichick is a phenomenon on par with Alex Ferguson. Unlike the Premier League, where wealth buys success, the draft continually works to rebuild the worst teams and to gently restrain the best. It's doesn't prevent dynasties, but it makes them less likely and less long-lived and, above all, it shows, unmistakably, who the great managers and the well-run clubs are.

Tellingly, Belichick's boss, the New England owner Robert Kraft, turned down the chance to buy Liverpool some years ago. Despite having been a founder of the MLS (he owns New England Revolution) and a lifelong football fan, he decided not to buy the club because, in his view, running a Premier League club well is no guarantee of success.

'In the end I want to be able to compete at the highest level,' he told British NFL journalist Neil Reynolds in 2012. 'And just look at what's happened this year with Manchester City. They're going to lose £100m but they won the championship. And I look at Chelsea and I didn't want to be in a league where I can't compete on management. I thought, no matter how good an operator I am, or how good we were at picking talent, I don't want to be in a business where people can just throw money [about].'[16]

So there we have it. The owner of the best-run club, with the best manager in the NFL, turned down the chance to buy one of the most famous football teams in the world because he couldn't see the point in trying to compete in the Premier League as it is. Smart man.

And that, sadly, is why Liverpool – let alone Aston Villa or Fulham – aren't going to win the title any time soon.

Meanwhile, Hoddle's team of immortals exist only in a parallel universe, powered by the willingness of a different set of football gods to share success. Perhaps, if he's good, we may all one day live to see the Promised Land, where the last shall be first and the first last.

It won't be the Kingdom of Hodd. It'll be the first draft of a new Premier League.

12.

'This guy's got a rocket-booster strapped to his back!'

Because there's room for the big guys.

IT'S a Tuesday afternoon in June 2062 and Steven Gerrard has almost finished mating. 'Hurry up, Steve,' bellows his agent, standing next to the bed, examining the schedule that's being projected on to his retina, 'you've another two need covering this afternoon.'

A few hours later, the recently retired Steven Gerrard III (to give him his full name) is dressing after unmounting his 12th model of what has been a busy week. His agent shakes his hand and bids him farewell with what Stevie-3, as he is popularly known, thinks of as unusual formality. A few minutes after that, as he leaves the hotel, Liverpool's former captain is bundled screaming into the back of a white van and driven away to be euthanised. Football is an unforgiving game.

'Hold still, Steven. This won't take a minute.'

Ask anyone, anywhere in the world, any time in the last 30 years, how the British play football and they will tell you: aggressive, muscular, hard-running, direct and full of heart. What they lack in skill they (almost) make up for in athleticism.

People of the world, have you not heard of Micky Quinn? Are Neil Ruddock and Gary Mabbutt new names to you? Have you never laid eyes – in widescreen – on Paul Gascoigne, Matthew Le Tissier or Neville Southall?

While the stereotype of the high-tempo British game is now largely true, when it was imprinted, British football was still filled with wildly unfit, overweight players, many of whom seemed better suited to a career at the oche than across the touchline. Every team had its own Kevin Pressman, Darren Caskey or James Beattie. And, while they'd get plenty of stick, these barrel-chested chubsters were often lionised (it is, after all, no mean feat to train three or four times a week, play at least one match, and yet still be overweight). In every one of these tubby wonders, with their complete refusal to conform to the requirements of their profession, there lurked the anarchic spirit of Randle McMurphy, mocking our ludicrous over-investment in the game.

Now, however, there is a fetishisation not just of fitness, but of athleticism. The slim, rangy, quick player beloved of Arsene Wenger has become the ideal modern footballer. It's a form of Total Football for fitness where every player, whatever their position, must be fast, lean and able to run for 90 minutes.

And who could argue with that? Greater fitness should provide faster, more spectacular football with fewer mistakes in the final 20 minutes of games.

A player must never harm Arsene or, through inaction, allow any harm to come to Arsene.

Except there's something quite anaemic about this vision. It's the basketballisation of football, with squads of almost interchangeable athletes bombing up and down the pitch continuously; the subtle rhythms of the old game replaced by the all-action, pell-mell heroics of pass-and-move endurance-bots.

I don't argue for tolerating lazy players but it would be a shame, I think, if some of our more mercurial talents, the ones born with the skill but not the physical ability to work wonders for more than 60 minutes, found themselves with no place in the game. When players have no weaknesses, when they bring 21st-century diet and training and equipment to 19th-century games, it is blandness, not greatness, that ensues.

Historically, team selection was a much more interesting and complex business than it is now. With more physically limited players and fewer substitutions, a manager had to work much harder to produce a matchday squad capable of adapting to the many different situations it might encounter.

Now a manager can pick any team he likes, confident that his seven substitutes can cover any eventuality. It's a shame because, while football has always sought to put out a starting 11 who can run all day, it's only with modern training methods and a global pool of talent that the game can now begin to eliminate the need for situational contributors.

The tall striker who can shake up the defence. The luxury winger who is replaced by a ball-winner away from home. The former midfielder who can drop back into a sweeper role. The chunky schemer who can pry open a defence. All these niches and more are vanishing and being replaced by a homogenised, slimline player, with a body type that bears as much relationship to a football fan as catwalk models do to your average Top Shopper.

There is a certain kind of sports fan you should never trust: the person who likes only one sport – usually it will be football, rugby or Formula 1 (if that were a sport[31]) – and dismisses all other sports, especially American football. All discerning sports fans should, I think, have a basic understanding and appreciation of the NFL, just as they should know a little about handball, track cycling and long-distance running.

---

31 Which it isn't. To me, a sport must:

1. Rely solely on human power (cycling, naturally, but it's goodbye to all motorsport).
2. Demand a level of extreme physical prowess such that performance peaks in the late 20s and players over 40 should not normally be able to compete at the top level (no golf, then).
3. Demand regular, strenuous movement and/or concentrated bursts of great strength – hand-eye coordination alone isn't enough (discus and javelin are in, but shooting, archery and, sacrilege, darts are out).
4. Have a scoring system determined in real-time, according to objective criteria, with a referee's job to confirm or deny a score, rather than to give a subjective value to an action (no diving, synchronised swimming, gymnastics and, yes, no boxing).
5. Amateur participation, even in some simplified form, shouldn't be cost prohibitive, especially for children. (There was no touch polo or five-a-side yachting at my school.)

As if they were wearing a jester's hat at a festival, these thick-headed chauvinists freely advertise their own inanity the moment American football is mentioned. Like a paid controversialist baiting their audience, out will come the jibes about fat men in pads, endless advertising breaks and the logical flaw in proclaiming someone world champion in a US-only sport.[32]

These and many other common disparagements of the game are, like the person who describes football as just '22 men kicking a ball around', technically correct but woefully lacking in perspective.

For the first 50 or so years of its existence, many American footballers played multiple roles on both the offence and defence. Since the second half of the 20th century, though, there's been an ever greater focus on specialisation, making the NFL far less of an athletic, endurance sport and far more explosive and power-based. As a consequence, your typical NFL team is far more diverse physically than a football team, creating opportunities for people of all shapes and sizes – including fat men in pads – to contribute.

Compare Denver and Arsenal, respectively the two most dangerous and exciting attacking teams in the 2013/14 NFL and Premier League seasons. If you plot the height, weight and BMI of each squad you see how homogenous football is compared to the NFL.

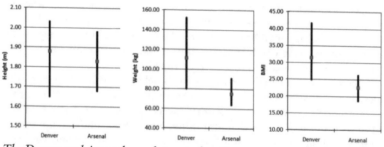

The Denver and Arsenal squads in numbers.[33]

It's no surprise that, as a squad, Denver were taller on average than Arsenal – under Wenger that have always tended to be one of the shorter Premier League clubs. But the NFL also allows room for some smaller players. If this had been a graph of Denver's team the previous season, it would've included 5ft4 Trindon Holliday, giving Denver players both taller and shorter than any member of the Arsenal squad.

In the weight category, again, as you would expect, Denver was much, much heavier: your average Arsenal player weighed only two thirds of your average Denver player. The heaviest Arsenal player (Mertesacker) would've been in

---

32 I've no actual evidence that, say, Jeremy Clarkson, James Delingpole, Rod Liddle and Toby Young don't like American football, but that won't stop me getting provocatively angry about it.

33 Calculations include all 53 members of Denver's active roster at 31st December 2014 and all 31 players listed in Arsenal's first team on the same date. Weights and heights from Denver official website and PremierLeague.com.

the lightest quarter of the Denver locker-room. And 15 Denver players – 28 per cent of their squad – weighed more than double that of Arsenal's lightest player (Alexis Sánchez). Finally, convert the weight and height to BMI, and you find that every single Denver was classed as either overweight or obese.

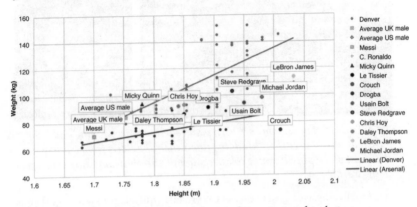

Confirmation that the author doesn't have a degree in graphic design.

Plot all the weights and heights and you can see a clear divide between the Arsenal and Denver team. Interestingly, add in a few other footballers and you'll see that, whether it's little Leo Messi, rangy Cristiano Ronaldo or lumbering Didier Drogba, they'd all broadly fit the height-weight ratio of the Arsenal squad.

If we want sportspeople who might have the heft for the NFL, we have to look for some of the bulkier footballers – Micky Quinn and Matthew Le Tissier – or cast the net wider to other sports. When he was competing, Steve Redgrave, Britain's greatest ever Olympian, was an almost perfect match in height and weight terms for Peyton Manning, Denver's all-time-great quarterback. Matt Le Tissier, meanwhile, had a similar height and weight (if not speed) to veteran Denver cornerback Champ Bailey. See if you can tell them apart.

'Looking good, Matt.' 'Feeling good, Champ.'

'Be not afraid of pads: some are born padded, some grow padding and some have pads thrust over their heads to protect their shoulders from trauma in the midst of the fastest, most explosive, most physically demanding team sport in the world.'

Finally, the average British male is broadly equivalent to wee Wes Welker – a dynamic player who, despite being generally regarded as a bit of a titch, takes fearsome punishment every week. Again, the resemblance is uncanny.

Of course, unlike your average British male, what Welker – along with his colleagues – is carrying around with him is mostly huge amounts of muscle rather than fat. So the BMI obesity tag doesn't quite fit, except at the top end, where the offensive and defensive linemen have both muscle and fat in extreme amounts.

These remarkable human beings need the speed, reach and power of heavyweight boxers as well as the balance, agility and footwork of wrestlers or taekwondo masters. Depending on whether they are on the offence or the defence, they spend the entire game either fighting to protect/kill the quarterback, or knocking their opponent out of the way to open/close a space for a runner. It's brutal, exhausting and should be recognised as a martial art in its own right.

And, despite their great bulk, linemen are capable of remarkable physical feats. Unlike football where players like Sheringham, Le Tissier or Micky Quinn got by on touch and anticipation, physical excellence is always demanded of NFL players.

Fire up YouTube again and take a look at one of the most famous plays in NFL history. Search for 'Larry Allen + Darion Conner'. Its star is the aforementioned Larry Allen of Dallas, one of the greatest offensive linemen of all time. In the film, the quarterback's pass is intercepted by an opposition player who, given where he catches it, would usually return the ball to the opposition's endzone and score a touchdown. I say usually, because the only players fast enough to stop him are the wide receivers who are most likely too far downfield to catch him. Everybody else – the tight ends, linemen, running back and quarterback – will be facing the wrong way and, in the case of the running back and quarterback, will stand little chance of bringing down a man the size of a heavyweight boxer as he flies past them.

And yet, this time, something incredible happens. Larry Allen, the battleship in silver, white and blue, wearing number 73 and weighing 23st, turns and, from a standing start, catches the ball-carrier, making a touchdown-saving tackle on the sidelines. Allen's speed is astonishing even before I tell you that the person he catches, Darion Conner, was the second fastest 100m runner in Mississippi in his school year.

A lovely measure of the greatness of a sporting achievement is the extent to which it turns professional commentators back into fans. Think of any of Barry Davies's best work. Or re-watch the footage of Odell Beckham Jr's famous catch in November 2014 – you can hear Cris Collinsworth become a dizzy school kid. 'Did he catch that?!' he gasps. 'Oh my goodness!'

In Larry Allen's case, initially the commentators can manage nothing more coherent then just shouting his name. Eventually they compose themselves a little. 'I can't believe that! Give me a break!...This guy's got a rocket-booster strapped to his back!'

Most of the time, such athleticism among the NFL's bigger players isn't visible, hidden as it usually is among a tangle of rucking bodies. But make no mistake, it's there. They are big, but they are awesome physical specimens.

Want further proof? Then welcome, if you please, J.J. Watt, the 6ft 5in, 21st Houston defensive lineman. Google for it and you can see Watt, without a run-up, jumping five feet vertically and landing on a box.

Do try this at home. No, really, give it a go. He makes it look so easy that it's easy to miss how staggeringly impressive it is. So, stop reading, go to your kitchen, open a cupboard door – the one above the kettle where you keep the teabags – and see if you can hop into it. Good luck.

Most NFL linemen are not as quick and explosive as Allen or Watt, of course, but they are a reminder that the NFL isn't just a leader in racial diversity, it's a sport that has room for almost any shape or size of athlete to excel. The game is full of people who could've been sprinters, baseball players, wrestlers, basketballers, boxers, discus throwers.

Football, meanwhile, had got that bit duller, that bit greyer, as the journeymen, the misshapes, the chancers, the strollers and the freaks have got weeded out. What's left is magnificent...but, somehow, it's not football.

Or at least it's not football with a smile on its face and a spring in its step. It's football devoid of fun; a game taking itself epically seriously in an effort to be seen as an industry.

First time round, Mario Balotelli was, by a mile, the best thing to happen to the Premier League in recent years. It shouldn't need explaining; he just was. So it reflects badly on the game that he was sent packing so quickly.

His departure, like so many other interestingly flawed players, is part of the ongoing loss of footballing biodiversity that made the game so rich and exciting. It's an extension of the ruthless logic – the puritan narrowness – of economic efficiency that's closing high streets, exporting manufacturing jobs and closing libraries. Money preaches choice but demands conformity.

Football has lost itself in the belief that everything must be ever faster and more streamlined. Gone is a thriving and varied player gene pool and, in its place, we have identikit tattooed greyhounds.

Generations from now, when we're genetically engineering Steven Gerrard's grandchildren to help produce the perfect attacking midfielder, we'll realise that, like racehorses and pedigree dogs, we've created an entire profession of athletes who look magnificent, but are intellectually and morally enfeebled by in-breeding. Prone to neurosis and double-footed tackles, weak of hamstring and utterly unable to cope in the real world, each season's end will see the class of newly washed-up players sent, not to the MLS to live out their remaining years in prosperous retirement, but to the car park where a vet will destroy them humanely.

Eventually, like Crufts, no one will want to acclaim the spectacle of dumb beasts suffering such cruelty.

The big guys, meanwhile, will still be kicking arse in the NFL.

13.

'He would have to be on the programme to tell me exactly what he was thinking there.'

Because their analysts tell you things you didn't already know.

NINETY per cent of everything is crap. So said Theodore Sturgeon, the fitfully brilliant author of *More Than Human*, when he was tired of people dismissing his work simply because it was science fiction. Yes, most science fiction is crap, he argued in what he called 'Sturgeon's Revelation', but since most movies, literature and products are crap too, a brilliant practitioner in one field need feel no shame about the failures of his or her fellow professionals. For this reason, Gary Neville, you can skip this chapter; the intellectually subnormal level of football broadcasting is not your fault.

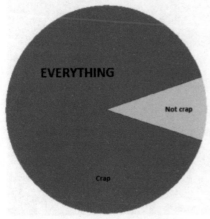

I prefer to call it 'Sturgeon's Underestimate'.

Saturday 19 October 2013 was a special day for me: I had a revelation of my own. I can trace its origins to Bill Barnwell, the brilliant US sportswriter whose 'Thank you for not coaching' column I'd been gorging on during the season. Published on Tuesdays, Barnwell would take apart the best and worst tactical decisions of the previous weekend's NFL games in forensic detail. If you have a passing interest in the sport, you needed absorb only a couple of these pieces to realise, as I did, that too often I was watching games to pass the time, rather than really engaging with their intricacies.

But back to my revelation. I was at home and, as I've done most Saturday evenings over the last 25 years, I switched on *Match of the Day*. It was then that it hit me: the realisation that not only did I never listen to a word Hansen, Lineker and Shearer said, but I literally couldn't remember when I last did.

Which would be the more surprising realisation? The sudden awareness that you are deaf? Or the immediate subsequent realisation that you don't remember the last time you heard anything?

An immaterial and insubstantial presence.

Confounded, I decided to watch a whole episode of *Match of the Day*. And I don't just mean sticking around until the last runt-of-the-litter 0-0 at the end. I mean actually listening, attentively, to every part of the commentary and analysis.

At first, I was a little excited by the prospect. I mean, I was sure Gary, Al and Al would have been keeping up with the latest trends in sports broadcasting, right? They'd have seen how Gary Neville throws down on Sky and incorporated some of it, no doubt?

You'd have thought.

It was like finding someone who's been lost in the wilderness with only foraged berries and tree bark to eat and taking them to a Little Chef for their first taste of real food.

Before his pay cut, Alan Hansen was on a reported £1.5m a year.[17] The magic of the internet helped me calculate that if he got paid in £20 notes, Hansen's annual pre-tax income from the BBC would be a pile of currency weighing 81.75kg.[18] That's about 12.75st which, given Hansen's height, means he was taking home about his own body weight in cash each year. For comparison, if you were on the then UK average income of £26,500, your wad would've weighed just 1.44kg – about a bag and a half of sugar.[19]

Alan Hansen in wardrobe, preparing for show time.[34]

---

34 Note to people who work at the BBC: you are custodians of what, with the NHS, is one of the last great things about Britain; the only two relics of a more civilised world, bulwarks against the Mongol Hordes of fundamentalist capitalism. Everything you do – every minor decision – is subject to scrutiny and any mistake could be used by media owners in their quest to make the UK an English-speaking Switzerland. So, for Christ's sakes, don't make it easy on them. Don't hand the tabloids a big stick and invite them to batter your employer with it. When you overpay bad presenters (sack Kirsty Wark!) or dumb-down programmes (sack the producer of *Question Time*!) or employ Alan Yentob (Alan Yentob, sack Alan Yentob!) or bury stories about Jimmy Savile, you don't just make a professional mistake, you do bring us one step closer to the precipice. So think hard, show some courage, strive for greatness and remember that, once the BBC's gone, it's never coming back. If you aren't up to this challenge, then bugger off to ITV. Thank you for your attention.

With this in mind, the next day, I transcribed the analysis so I could read and re-read the wisdom of Lineker, Hansen and Shearer to see what, if anything, they add to the programme. I did this tentatively with a view to pulling together a review of a whole season of the show.

As it turns out, this wasn't necessary. Gathering the awesome tsunami of banalities that follow didn't require exhaustive research. All it took was that one episode, randomly chosen. All it took was that one episode, randomly chosen.[20] Come and relive it with me…

The headline game of the day is Chelsea's 4-1 victory over Cardiff. The key incident was, apparently, the mistaken decision of the referee not to give a foul when Eto'o robbed the Cardiff keeper, David Marshall, allowing Hazard to score. In a post-match interview with Malky Mackay, who lucidly reported his conversation with the referee's assistant, the relevant law is quickly established (a ball being bounced is considered under the keeper's control, as if he were holding it in both hands, and is therefore off limits). This produces the incontestable conclusion that the goal shouldn't have stood.

Despite this – despite it already being completely clear that this was a costly mistake – the goal is still picked over in detail as the first item in the brief studio analysis. Only then do we move to the rest of the game. All the quotes that follow are verbatim. I've edited in square brackets only where I think the absence would render the quotes unintelligible.

Hansen, 'Chelsea ran out easy winners in the end. But this is a sensational goal.' [Clip plays of Eto'o's goal.] 'Great first touch there, Al…'

Shearer, 'Brilliant…'

Hansen, 'Great goal…'

Shearer, 'Long time coming…'

Hansen, 'Well absolutely. They run out easy winners, but it was 1-0 at the time when the referee gave a bad decision.'

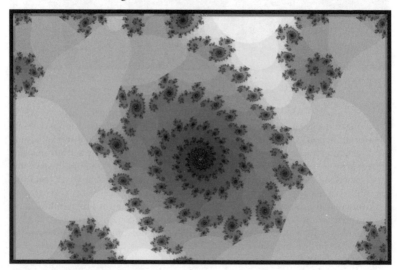

Match of the Day *at x100 magnification.*

Incidentally, you'll note already the first indication of *Match of the Day*'s fractal nature. Any piece of the show, seen at any order of magnitude, contains the shape of the whole. Shearer is there at every pause, like a touring backing singer for Guns N' Roses, providing breathy woos, ahhs and other inconsequential vocal trills to smooth out the grating sound of the frontman performing live. Hansen, meanwhile, was a man who used the word 'sensational' so often that he sounded like some aging libertine, his body so wracked with decades of numbing perversions that he has to swallow a handful of Viagra with his morning coffee to continue his quest for ever-stronger and more dangerous footballing thrills.

So, with the question of the refereeing mistake doubly solved, and all goals suitably praised, our team move on to a discussion of the performance of David Luiz. Demonstrating just how good Harry Hill really is, Hansen voices over a series of clips of Luiz's mistakes.

Hansen, 'Casual. Takes too many chances. Always a mistake in there.' Yes, it takes a former pro turned top analyst to spot that here is a man prone to error.

We see a bad tackle, a misdirected pass. Hansen, 'He gives the ball away. Well, what's that all about?' You tell us Alan. Go on, explain what he does well or why managers keep picking him. That's your job.

Then we see Luiz leaving a ball he clearly needs to get, with Jordon Mutch running on to it and scoring. Again, Hansen is surgical. 'I've never seen anything like it. It's just, what is he doing? He would have to be on the programme to tell me exactly what he was thinking there.'

'You thought it was going to run through to the keeper, didn't you? Am I right?'

Why bother with analysts if, like Hansen – who appeared to be struggling with the hard problem of consciousness – they have nothing to say?

If you watch the NFL, where they have to be able to give trenchant analysis *between each play*, if you listen to Cris Collinsworth or download Ross Tucker or Matt Williamson or read Mike Carlson, you can learn the complexities of the NFL piece by piece. In contrast, you could watch *Match of the Day* for the rest of eternity and still know nothing other than what a goal looks like or when you should award a penalty, flag for offside or produce a red card.

So, with the first game – the match of the day? – autopsied with carcass largely intact, we still know nothing of what worked tactically nor what we have learned about the teams and their progress. Except for this gem.

Hansen, 'I think they're back in business. Looking at the personnel they play and the personnel they left out, I think they'll be there or thereabouts.'

Warming to his role as a human echo chamber, Shearer murmurs, 'Improvingly rapidly...'

Next up, it's the Liverpool–Newcastle game. When we come back to the studio, before the analysis, Lineker informs us that Steven Gerrard has become only the sixth midfielder to score 100 Premier League goals. This remarkable achievement, signifying an extraordinary club career, is greeted thus:

> Lineker, 'What a record, Steven Gerrard. What a player over so many years. One hundred goals. Congratulations.'
> Hansen, 'Well done.'

And that's it; Steven Gerrard's milestone fully contextualised and appreciated. He may not quite have become the world-class player we all desperately hoped he would, but he was a magnificent player for Liverpool and he deserved a better tribute than that shoddy effort.

This brief segment typifies the deep-seated laziness, compliancy and intellectual deficiency of modern football broadcasting. I can't imagine that there's a football fan in the land who couldn't have found *something* to say about Gerrard, yet Lineker, despite over a decade fronting the premier review programme of the world's richest league, is apparently unable to talk interestingly off-the-cuff and unwilling to put in the time to prepare.

Next it's time for our panel's thoughts on the game. A graphic reading 'analysis' appears, presumably because 'voiceover for the blind' wouldn't have fitted.

Discussing (of course) the sending-off of a player, Hansen tells us, 'It was ironic, because until then they'd done so well. It was the first time they'd actually left space in behind. And Suarez, a little bit of movement there. You know, the defender comes in. He's got no chance, Al, has he really?'

> Shearer, 'Well, what I love about Tioté. Tioté is carrying an injury. If you watch, he's the one who actually plays everyone, er, Suarez, onside.'
> We freeze frame and a line is telestrated, showing the last man when the ball was played.

Shearer, 'It's a lovely ball. A lovely run. But what Suarez does very cleverly is get his first touch right and then get his body across him. So he has to foul him and it's really good centre-forward play. And if you look what happens in an identical position to Remi [footage of a similar situation for the Newcastle forward], Škrtel gets the tackle in, but he's got to use his body there. Got to get that ball away from Škrtel and get his body across him and if he does try and touch him, he's got to foul him and bring him down. And just look at Suarez here, last minute of the game. Talk about using your body, it's very clever centre-forward play 'cause Debuchy's getting the tackle in. If he's gonna hit the ball, he got to take him out first and it was a foul. Good play.'

Hansen, 'And he was terrific in the match, Suarez.'

While we're struggling to get our heads around this torrent of insight, we see graphics showing post-match tweets from players. One, purporting to be from Glen Johnson, reads, 'Great to be back. Shame we couldn't get all 3 points. Another week now to get the fitness back.'

Was this really Glen Johnson or a Turing test candidate created by a nine-year-old computer prodigy with an interest in football? Surely there's no way Glen Johnson, a millionaire so cost conscious that he once tried to steal a toilet seat, would waste his valuable time tweeting this to his 840,000 followers?[21] And even if he did think this thought – and think it worth sharing – what on earth were the producers doing thinking the viewers might be edified by it?

'Don't worry about going shopping mum, Glen says he can get us a great deal...'

Back to Shearer, 'Newcastle got hammered six by Liverpool not that long ago. They were significantly better this time.' This game ended 2-2, so well-spotted, Alan.

Hansen, 'I actually thought Newcastle defensively were magnificent. Went down to ten men [we see footage of last season]. This was last year. Shambolic. All over the place. Left so much space in behind. Worst thing that can happen is if you virtually [let the opposition] walk the ball into the back of the net. That was Sturridge to Henderson. This time, again, they're pushing up, trying to hold the line. Get it totally wrong. Loads of space in behind. Gerrard over the top. Oceans of space to go in there. Henderson this time to Sturridge. Today you didn't see that at all.'

Lineker, 'What was different?'

Good question, Gary! Having watched the show several times, this is the one occasion he made any kind of acceptable contribution to audience enlightenment. So, let's see if the answer helps us understand the relative changes in the performance and approaches of the teams since they last met.

Hansen, 'Well, they just defended deeper. They defended; were organised. Defended deeper, defended the sanctuary of the 18-yard line. And when they got it, they picked it up and played it. And, to be fair they limited Liverpool to only one or two very, very good chances. Again, this was it. The same sort of thing. Men behind the ball [sadly, not with jumpers for goalposts]. No space in behind. And then, what was impressive in the second half was they, when they did get men behind the ball and they got it, they did break. And they broke with great conviction. And this is Remi, and Liverpool streaming back, four or five, to try and get back there. And Newcastle had one or two good opportunities and I thought tactically very, very astute, Pardew.'

There we have it. The difference between losing six-nil and getting a draw is breaking with conviction and defending the sanctuary of the 18-yard line, two curious pieces of language that hint at a deeper spiritual purpose to Hansen's 20 years of exposing diabolical mistakes. Notably, too, we have the first use of the word 'tactics' – only 29 minutes and ten seconds into the programme.

Compare Hansen's analysis of Newcastle's improvements – which he's had hours to prepare – with Cris Collinsworth's almost instantaneous reaction to an improvised run by Aaron Rodgers in an NFL game broadcast the same week. Less than five seconds after the Green Bay quarterback has been wrestled to the ground by a Minnesota player, we see a replay showing the last-ditch efforts of the Green Bay offensive linemen to protect Rodgers from the stronger, faster defenders they were facing.

Collinsworth, 'Boy! Just good enough from Don Barclay on the outside. One final push [on the defender] and you see that little opening to the right. Typically, when you have a four-man rush, there is at least one gap that will open.' Aaron Rodgers then sees it and takes off.

With zero preparation time, Collinsworth has told us how Rodgers escaped, that the offensive line only just held up and that, other things being equal, the defensive formation has a flaw that can be exploited (this example, along with the others cited, comes solely from live coverage of the first quarter of one NFL game, again chosen at random). A few minutes later, Rodgers produces an important pass to keep Green Bay moving. Instantly, Collinsworth tells us not just what happened, but what Rodgers was thinking, how the pass was executed and that, again, the Minnesota defence has an exploitable flaw.

Collinsworth, 'Well, the quickness of the release is much of the magic. That time the [Minnesota] Vikings try and come with the blitz. Doesn't take Aaron Rodgers long to figure that out. Just gives a little back shoulder [pass] out there. And if the Vikings have an issue, it's been trying to play that straight bump-and-run, man-to-man coverage on the outside. And, so far tonight, they're not winning that battle either.'

Put these extemporised explanations side-by-side with the prepared output of football analysts, and you'll see that, at a simple level, far more valuable information is being imparted. Having watched both sports regularly for years, it's hard for me to avoid the conclusion that NFL commentators work harder, prepare better, face higher expectations and communicate more articulately than anyone covering football on TV not named Gary Neville.

Returning to the programme: at this point I was fulminating against Hansen. What's the point of an analyst who tells us only what we can already see? But, as the show went on, my attention began to shift.

Bad as Hansen was, with his exhausted tape-loop of clichés, and bad as Shearer is, with his phatic close-harmony endorsements of the banal, Lineker takes bad to a whole different plane. He's gives a competent performance when reading links – and he tweets some pretty trenchant stuff on occasions – but, despite decades as a broadcaster, he seems completely unable to chip in intelligently. It's quite something when you consider he played for Gordon Milne, Howard Kendall, Terry Venables, Luis Aragonés, Johan Cruyff and Sir Bobby Robson.

This was Lineker's contribution when teeing up our panel to discuss the goalscoring performance of Paul Dummett, who was making only his second appearance for Newcastle. It is one of the great, penetrating footballing questions of our time.

> Lineker, 'Today, I think 28 per cent possession for Newcastle in the second half, which you'd expect with ten men...er, Paul Dummett?'
> Hansen, 'Well...'
> Shearer, 'Brilliant for him. Local lad. Coming through. It's hard enough coming on, the job he has to do, when they've only got ten men, but his movement here is brilliant. He runs away from everyone, comes to the far post, no one follows him...'

We then cut to other footage from the game, with Dummett defending. Hansen, 'I hate doing this, but cardinal sin. Get your hand up. Looks across at the linesman. If he doesn't do that and tracks back...'

Shearer, for once not just quietly parroting Hansen, smiles back with the comradely indulgence of a business executive talking shop while a lap dancer gyrates in front of him and his colleagues. 'Don't spoil his day. He's had a big day. He scored. Why do you have to pick him up for that?'

'There's three guys back there say they know John Motson.'

After that 40-watt segment, it's time for Arsenal against Norwich, a game that finished 4-1. Immediately after we return to the studio, familiar Hansen themes emerge.

Hansen, 'The first game of the season, it was a shambles. They've now got an embarrassment of riches. He's got a lovely problem of who he's going to pick and who he's going to leave out.'

My god, people actually do speak like this. Well, on British football coverage they do. On Channel 4, between plays, Mike Carlson is discussing whether promising but unconventional college quarterback Johnny Manziel will be able to make it in the NFL.

Carlson, 'If you're old enough to remember "Pistol Pete" Maravich [a basketball player who retired in 1980]; when I watch Manziel playing football, that's what I think of. He's a guy who just does things you don't expect a quarterback should be able to do. It's like watching a Harlem Globetrotter playing a competitive game. Sometimes it's like he's got the ball on a little string and he's pulling it back...'

Guest analyst Rocky Boiman chimes in, 'I have a feeling that when coaches watch Manziel that they go "Oh no!... Don't... Oh, nice play!" He just creates and invents all the time.'

After a brief discussion of Tim Tebow, a player with similarities to Manziel who failed in the NFL, Carlson returns, 'In the NFL, you have to be consistent, you have to make the simple plays consistently well. And when you see a guy making loads of spectacular plays, you think, "Can he make simple plays?"'

Like Collinsworth, without preparation, Carlson has elegantly explained why many NFL coaches were lukewarm on a player who appeared to the untrained eye to be the NFL equivalent of Mario Balotelli: at the highest level of sport, a professional coach won't keep his job for long if his game plan depends on improvised brilliance.[35]

Back in Salford, our panel now run through Wenger's possible strongest 11 as a way of leading into a discussion of Aaron Ramsey. By the way, this next section is best read in the voice of three 12-year-old girls flicking through the new One Direction annual.

> Geri Lineker, '...Aaron Ramsey...'
> Ally Shearer, 'Sensational isn't he?'
> Alexia Hansen, 'Ugghhh! I mean, he came off the bench today and I mean this is the cut back for Özil. Timed to perfection but, and I love this; we were drooling about this. This is like Zidane, wasn't it? It was like... unbelievable...'
> Ally, 'Technique is just brilliant...'
> Alexia, 'Sensational...'
> Ally, 'He just looks so comfortable on the ball. So much confidence in his game.' [Isn't that what we all dream of, girls? A man who's confident on the ball?]
> Alexia, 'Here you are, look at this. Everything he's trying is coming off. But the goal is absolutely sensational as well. He's got so much confidence. He's obviously got half a yard of pace and he's got the strength to go with it. And he's always had the technique. This again. Wilshere picks it up. It's a great first touch. He sells him dummy after dummy after dummy and dispatches it into the back of the net. But, to beat that...'
> Geri, 'How good is this goal!?' [Continues, breathlessly, like this for some time...]

Later, when discussing the Manchester United v Southampton draw, there's the first hint that some effort or preparation has gone into the show, with Shearer unveiling some quite interesting statistics.

---

35 Carlson was speaking in late October 2013. By the time the draft came around the following May, many teams appeared to feel as Carlson did, with Manziel – despite being one of the most famous sportspeople in the US – not being selected until Cleveland took him with the 22nd pick. Manziel then failed to win the starting quarterback job from the player he drafted to replace and, at the time of writing this chapter, he hadn't started a single one of Cleveland's first 11 games. He'll get a shot eventually – first round draft picks are like club record signings – but it's far from certain what he'll do with it when he does.

'My god, his head is so shiny!'

Shearer, '[They have the] best defensive record in the league. [They've] conceded three goals. This time last year, after eight games, [they'd] conceded 24...'

Shearer then shows footage of Southampton playing further up the field and being more aggressive with their formation. But this flicker of insight is soon extinguished and, after a decent West Ham–Manchester City game and a Swansea thrashing of Sunderland, we plunge into the tedium of Everton v Hull. Not even Lineker can detract from that.

The final match of the night is the Stoke–West Brom 0-0. After a few minutes of lowlights, the analysis is wrapped up:

> Lineker, 'Stoke can't score.'
> Shearer, 'They can't score, they can't score at all. But they've got a hell of a good goalkeeper and that's what you need when you're not scoring. He's playing well, isn't he?'
> Lineker, 'And that's the key...'

Yes, indeed, Gary, that's the key. Playing well, getting men behind the ball, not letting in goals, being sensational, attacking in numbers, defending in numbers, getting your body between the man and the ball, playing with confidence, being clever, defending the sanctuary of the 18-yard line. These are the keys to the game.

You could argue that this is all gratuitous. So commentary is bad; who cares?

Well, at least with the politicians who let us down, we often suspect they are capable of more. Every news bulletin will have an interview with an obviously intelligent Member of Parliament saying something obviously untrue in lieu of actually trying to explain both the complexity of the situation and how their ideological underpinning guides their response to it.

'I say to the honourable gentleman, he will be disappointed not to have stuck that one away.'

But with football, we've put up with such poor analysis for so long that we've bred a generation of pundits who, if they lived in the US, wouldn't be able to get hired by a local paper to cover high school sports. And they, in turn, have perpetuated the poor level of understanding that prompts fans and chairmen to demand instant results and to be intolerant of any tactical innovation.

The Dunning-Kruger effect is a psychological flaw characteristic of people in which the least skilled are often most likely to express confidence in their ability. Conversely, those with the most knowledge are often found to have the greatest awareness of their limitations.

It affects us all – fans and *Match of the Day* presenters alike – and we must tackle it by demanding and being receptive to informed commentary.

I like to imagine that, if you questioned football fans worldwide, there would be an inverse relationship between international success and the professed level of knowledge of fans. Spanish fans, I fondly believe, would contain the fewest armchair managers.[36]

Given that it's probably untrue – that football coverage is bad the world over and that Sturgeon's Revelation applies as much to football fans as to science fiction – only one option remains: now Hansen has retired, we must sack Lineker and Shearer, and offer Gary Neville the run of the BBC sports department.

The future of English football, as well as my Saturday nights, depends on it.

---

36 Spanish sports coverage is not without its problems, however. For reasons real or imagined, Spanish TV networks believe their viewers are interested in a sporting competition only while Spain – or a Spanish player – is in with a shot at winning it. That doesn't sound like a particularly remarkable general statement of principle, but let me give you an example of how far sporting chauvinism can go. I was in Valencia the weekend that Andy Murray won Wimbledon. Now in Spain they love tennis. There's enormous participation at an amateur level and, in Rafael Nadal, they have a national hero and all-time great. However, with Nadal having gone out in the first round and David Ferrer exiting in the quarter-finals, and therefore no further Spanish interest, the tennis was simply yanked from the schedules. I had to 'watch' Murray's victory by hitting refresh on the BBC's ball-by-ball coverage online. The same will often happen late in the Tour de France if there's no longer a serious Spanish challenge, despite the country's powerful attachment to the sport.

14.

'A worthless trinket that will do nothing to feed my family.'

Because they share the TV money equally.

THE beautiful thing about sport is how it rewards you. Even if most of the time it feels like a rigged roulette wheel, play it for long enough and it will eventually pay you out with moments of personal and collective glory. These shining memories will warm you like winter sun and allow you to partake, Wilbur Mercer-like, of the real successes of the professional teams you support. So let's take a moment to celebrate you and *your* sporting career. Make a mental list of your top five greatest sporting achievements. Big or small, let it be the things that cheer you the most; the times you momentarily astonished the world with your brilliance.

What's on your list? When you nutmegged the rival school captain who went on to play professionally? Your last-minute bicycle kick off the line that preserved your team's lead in the cup final? The time you seven-balled a pool shark in front of all your friends?

This is real glory. This is why we play sport. Because, while winning isn't everything, winning *something* occasionally – no matter how small – is a glory that enriches our lives like love and friendship and art.

I have an idea for improving tennis. Well, I have several ideas – including making the court larger and abolishing second serves – but, for now, let me tell you about just one of them. It's a new way of allocating prizes. Here's how it works: at the end of each year, the top-ranked player on the tour will be given the best racket. Everyone else will have to play with decreasingly taut strings until those in the lower reaches of the top 100 will be swinging wildly with little more than butterfly nets.

And, to make it even better, the most famous and popular players will also be given the best tennis shoes. Everyone else will have to play in wedges, clogs or wellies. How do you like it?

5. Winning a cross country race at secondary school.[37]

For winning the Champions League in 2012/13, Bayern Munich received (earned is not, I think, quite the right word) more than £30m as well as a top-up of at least £16m, reflecting the size of the German TV market. Manchester United, however, who went out in the last 16, came away with just less than £30m. Don't worry, though, for winning the Premier League they pulled in a warmly consoling £60.8m.

In the same year, Baltimore won the Super Bowl. Their prize money? Nothing. That's right, while the players got win bonuses of about £50,000, the team took home not one extra dollar from one of the richest sporting and TV spectacles in the world. So angered by this unfairness were Baltimore that many players refused to celebrate. The winning coach even hurled the Vince Lombardi Trophy to the turf, refusing to handle what he described as a 'worthless trinket that will do nothing to feed my family'.

---

37 'Remember,' said the PE teacher, 'on the way back, we're finishing at the front gate.' Running in my breathless, stickman style – like an endurance walker who missed breakfast – I quickly lost sight of the leaders. Towards the end of the race, though, passing the back entrance to the school, I saw the ten people in front of me sitting on the steps of the sports hall, all having gone the wrong way. I put on a burst to distance myself from the other weaklings – the boys who, despite not being fat, still couldn't run – rounded the final corner and took the tape in front of a small but astonished crowd in the car park. Victory!

Baltimore struggles with the monumental injustice of just winning.

In fact, of course, he did no such thing. Somehow, using a reserve tank of sportsmanship untainted by avarice, the players, executives and fans of Baltimore were able to content themselves with the simple and unremunerated glory of being the 'world champions' of their sport. They managed, god knows how, to put the financial unfairness of it all behind them and enjoy the pure, exalted wonder of victory. As they should.

When it comes to prize money, the NFL, as in so many ways, is the oddball of world sport. What you get for winning is a trophy, no more. You've won, the thinking goes, what more could you want? Money? Well, if we gave you that as well, it would unfairly handicap the other teams and distort competition. And that would make the win less special if you managed to win again next year.[38]

Most sports, of course, don't take this view. And often it's not to the particular detriment of the game. In tennis, for example, there is extreme inequality in prize money. But it has to be recognised that, while a bigger share of the winnings might allow you more first-class travel and a better coach, what it buys – more than any competitive advantage – is simply a bigger house. In football, however, it buys you the equivalent of a bionic arm, a laser sight and rocket-powered trainers.

---

38 Teams have only won back-to-back Super Bowls on eight occasions, including three times since 1992/93. In the same period, teams won successive Premier League titles on three occasions (Manchester United twice and Chelsea). Ferguson's men also twice won the title three years on the bounce – making, effectively, seven Premier League retentions in just over two decades.

4. Drug cheating in a work five-a-side.[39]

You may be familiar with the 'ultimatum game', a thought experiment used by economists and game theorists to explore how unearned rewards are shared. It posits a situation where Player 1 is given a sum of money and must then offer some of that money to Player 2. If Player 2 accepts the offer, both parties keep their shares of the money. If Player 2 deems the offer insufficient, they may reject it, leaving both players with nothing.

Logically, Player 1 should try to keep as much money as possible and Player 2 should accept any offer, no matter how low. In practice, though, Player 1 will frequently offer a 50/50 split, while Player 2 will often reject anything worse than an 80/20 split.

How you see this experiment says much about your social and political perspective. Perhaps it's heartening that so many people are naturally generous and that others are prepared to tolerate some personal loss to teach a greedy person a lesson. Perhaps, though, it tells you that people are often unable to make rational decisions about their best interests and are too fearful of others' judgment to negotiate as hard as they should.

Thought experiments like this, or the more famous 'prisoner's dilemma', are often dismissed as being artificial on the grounds that these carefully contrived academic tools live in laboratories, shorn of much of the context inherent in human decision-making. But the real reason they are artificial is that, in the

---

39 In my first job, temping after university, my boss was a former amateur boxer. His dad was a trainer who also imported ephedrine illegally from Pakistan. One week, at the work football game, we took some and spent the evening bombing around like Ronaldo with a point to prove. It wasn't the winning that I remember and it certainly didn't make me better on the ball. But it meant I could run all night, that every run was a sprint and that, when I stopped, I could catch my breath instantly. When the game was over, I ran all the way home. For that one night, I had a sense of what it must feel like to have a body whose limits were far past those of ordinary mortals. I wish everyone could feel that way once.

real world, those who frame laws or tax codes or executive contracts or revenue sharing models, carefully avoid building in mechanisms that allow the weak to demand fairness on pain of punishment.

Take the Premier League. There the model is an adjusted (and instantly familiar) form of the ultimatum game in which the only power the poor clubs have, on receiving their meagre offer from the rich, is to reject their own stake. They can only prevent a deal if enough clubs are willing to band together to rewrite the rules, something procedurally possible but practically inconceivable since it would require at least some clubs to vote against their own financial interests and would risk the big clubs pressing the nuclear button they like to advertise before any big negotiation: a further breakaway league.

At its founding, the Premier League agreed to share TV money on the following principles:

- All international income (about 40 per cent of the total TV money) would be shared equally between the 20 teams.
- Fifty per cent of the UK TV revenue would be split equally between the 20 clubs.
- The remaining 50 per cent would be split in half and paid out according to final league position and the frequency with which that club is televised.[22]

And there, wrapped up in a formula that appears based on a fair distribution, is an inbuilt bias that substantially rewards the clubs who are more likely to win the league and be on TV. Constitutionally, in the Premier League the rich must get richer.

Leaving aside, for a moment, the question of equity, we need to ask how significant are these rewards for league position and TV popularity ('merit payments' and 'facility fees', as the Premier League refers to them)?

The answer is, apparently small in any given season but, cumulatively, huge. Here's the breakdown for TV income in 2011/12.

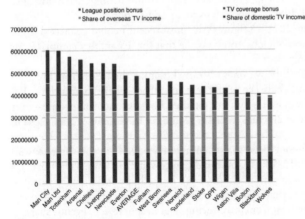

The real league table.

Even being Wolves – with £40m to spend – isn't too bad, is it? It's only £20m less than Manchester City. At least Wolves' donkeys were cheap; City had some really expensive ones to feed.

But look how the unequal distribution adds up over time. In the three seasons from 2010/11 to 2012/13, Manchester United got the highest TV income – a total of £181.59m. Wigan received the lowest of any of the 14 sides who appeared in all three Premier League campaigns, with £125m. That's £56.59m less than United. In other words, United received 45 per cent more TV income than Wigan in that three-year period.

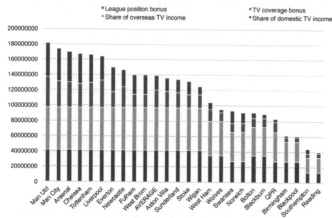

How the structure of revenue sharing rapidly amplifies financial inequality.

How significant is that difference? Well, for United, whose income in 2011/12 was £320m, it is tempting to say 'not very'. Not compared to someone like Wigan, whose income in 2011/12 was just £53m.

In fact, though, taken over the 21 years of the Premier League, what might appear as a relatively minor incentive element in the deal actually becomes a way of large clubs raking off a huge quantity of money, entrenching their dominance and putting small clubs in a precarious financial position.

Looking at the 2011/12 figures (the most recent I could get access to) to see what proportion of clubs' total income that the TV money comprises, its importance is amply clear.[23]

For the biggest clubs, the ones who are skimming the cream from the prize fund, TV contributes between 15 per cent and 30 per cent of their income. For the small clubs, though, it is by a margin their biggest source of income – over 50 per cent for 14 of 20 clubs in 2011/12 and, in the case of Wigan, close to 80 per cent.

Had all TV money been shared completely equally in the three seasons from 2010/11 to 2012/13, Wigan would've received £138.98m. That's an extra £13.98m – or £4.66m extra a season. Even in the hyperinflationary world of the Premier League, that is an important top-up. If you graph who would've benefited most and least from introducing an even split to TV revenue sharing, you see clearly that a small loss (in percentage of income) to the big teams –

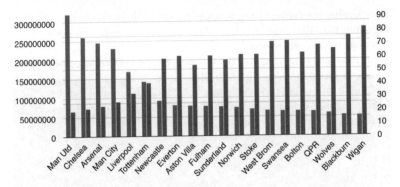

The Premier League's TV addiction in numbers.

which might merely take the edge off their ability to keep pushing up wages or transfer fees – could make a big difference to the actual financial viability of smaller clubs.

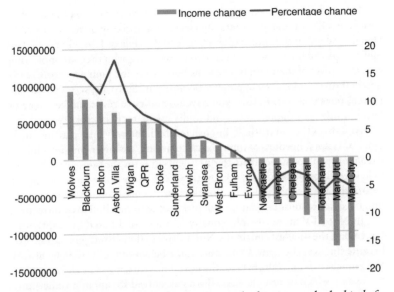

Note how all the clubs who'd lose under an equal split are exactly the kind of clubs who already have too much money.

Nonetheless, it won't happen. Who voluntarily surrenders their excessive slice of the pie so that all the little people can have a few crumbs more?

There's no point appealing to notions of fairness – nor even to the idea that quality of competition (and hence saleability of TV rights) demands a league full of quality opposition.

The simple fact is that Manchester United et al don't care about nurturing healthy competition. Quite the contrary, the last thing they want is small clubs joining the Premier League, growing, establishing themselves and then beginning to challenge for honours. What they want instead is cannon fodder: a rotating cast of teams prepared to be beaten weekly, fobbed off with a token for their efforts and then relegated with frequently ruinous financial consequences.

3. My greatest goalkeeping performance.[40]

For all the thought experiments in the game theory canon, the situation with football's TV money is actually closer to a drinking game described by Douglas Adams in the Hitch Hiker's Guide to the Galaxy. In it, a bottle of 'Janx Spirit' is placed on a table between two contestants, who then attempt, using only the power of their minds, to tip the bottle over and pour a measure of this potent intoxicant for their opponent. Because Janx Spirit 'depresses telepsychic power', once you start to lose, you have no ability to resist and you keep on losing, while your opponent sits and coldly calculates his victory.

And that's the sad truth: in English football, the only ones playing for the glory of victory, heedless of financial calculations, are lower-division clubs. A stream of small teams compete to ruin themselves for the honour of sharing a field with clubs who don't even know they exist, sadly unaware as they parade before the fans, sun blinded by the glory of the occasion, that they are not knights come to joust for honour, but just another dumb bull to be tormented.

In NFL, TV money is split equally 32 ways. As I noted in chapter one, Green Bay, the smallest club in the NFL by size of hometown population, exist because their get the same TV income as the behemoths of Dallas, New York, San Francisco or Pittsburgh. Over the next nine years, it will be about $137.5m per team – which means each club has a guaranteed stream of income almost exactly equivalent to the annual league salary cap. As a result, every single team can afford to compete for the best players and, with the impact of the draft, can hope to build a winning side.

---

40 I was nine and playing in goal (to minimise harm to the rest of the team). At half-time we were 3-0 down and I'd actually played pretty well. In the second half we scored four goals and I made save after save, including three one-on-ones with their three-goal striker. Even though a team-mate scored a hat-trick, including the winning goal, it was me who was carried from the field on the shoulders of my team-mates. I was unbeatable. Until the next week when we lost six-nil and I let two in through my legs.

2. Catching a baseball in San Francisco.[41]

Clubs aren't restrained from profit, of course. Whatever they can make from tickets they can keep. Dallas, meanwhile, are the only team to sell their own merchandise. The other 31 teams are content to pool merchandise income and share it equally. Either way, every NFL franchise is a goldmine.

What they don't seem to suffer in the NFL is the myth of the self-made man – the belief among the rich and powerful that they are the sole authors of their success.

He who accepts not just the trophy but also a greater share of the income, knowing it gives him a cumulative advantage, unconsciously or otherwise asserts his belief in his own natural superiority.

He is wrong, of course, but that's the wheedling, whining, self-pitying power of greed. It demands not just an ever greater share but an accompanying acknowledgement of its entitlement. It's why CEOs buy first big houses and

---

41 My wife and I were on a road trip through Southern California. Halfway through a poor game between the Giants and the Diamondbacks, two guys stormed out and, leaving, asked if we wanted their (better) tickets. We switched seats and moved closer to the action. Literally the next pitch, a lefty socked it directly at me, low and hard. Despite a wave of other fans pressing in, I caught it – and looked up to see myself grinning foolishly on the TV screen. There was cheering and clapping. When it became clear I was a tourist, one of the stewards began yelling, 'Check this man out! He's over from London, catches a ball in his first game!' Five minutes later, another ball came sailing high into our section. I went for it again but found myself outjumped by the guy beside me. It was a beautiful moment because this was the very same man who'd warmly and generously congratulated me for my catch, even though he'd been coming to games, he'd told me, for nearly 20 years and had never snagged one. He was even happier than I had been.

then honours and opera houses; why pop stars and actors want first fame and then respect.

Even a well-framed, balanced constitution isn't a complete bulwark against the perversion of decision-making by vested interests. Ultimately, the NFL owners continue to share because, as well as their inherited set of values, the game continues to produce a handsome profit for every owner.

1. Eight out at the work softball game.[42]

Sadly, in the Premier League, the big clubs didn't have to wrangle entrenched loyalties and attitudes, they simply wrote a constitution anew. In hindsight, as they sit, tipping the bottle again and again on their weaker opponents, and with the game plagued by reckless financial management and in thrall to the malignant morality of a winner-takes-all land grab, they probably think they were far too generous.

---

42 Primrose Hill: a strangely genteel place to clinch sporting immortality. Fielding on the boundary, I caught eight people out in one moderately contested, mixed ability, after-work game, including a high, diving catch behind my head that was, by a mile, the pinnacle of my sporting life. The moment the hardest guy in the office swung his bat and thundered it towards central London, I knew it was down to me. I broke from my crouch and began sprinting back and around to intercept the bazooka. I realised that, given what I'd done already in the game, everyone was watching, holding their breath. Even the batsman had stopped running, not even halfway to first, to stare. I didn't expect to get anywhere near it; its power and trajectory would take it well past me. I was tearing across the field. Everything went silent. My mind was clear. I launched myself full length to my right, back arched, arm extended. I collapsed in a heap, feeling my face pressed into the rough, brown grass and, when I raised my glove to signal I had the ball, people burst out cheering and clapping. This is not something to which I was or have ever become accustomed. I was only 23 years old. I waved proudly and trod in some dog shit.

The NFL has spent years monitoring the other big North American sports and carefully calibrating the likely impact of any structural changes on the game to ensure fairness of competition and parity of clubs is maintained. Here, there is no such prudent administration.

If you ask many football fans which league, outside of the Premier League, they most admire, the answer would likely be Spain's La Liga. Sadly, if you asked the owners of the Premier League's big clubs, the answer would probably be the same. For it is there, in La Liga, that clubs sell their own TV rights and Barca and Madrid take home almost half of the total pie [24] (although proposals are afoot to reduce their share).

It's time to remind ourselves, though, what the purpose of team sport is. It's to feel connected socially and, whether as a player or a fan, to share the experience of collective effort, collective achievement, collective improvement, collective failure. In among this selfless labour, there are a thousand opportunities for joyful moments of sporting success and, at the end of the season, there is the chance for one team to be crowned the ultimate winners.

Those who think themselves a more valuable cog – rather than just a bigger cog – in this wheel are mistaken. Just they are wrong when they see themselves as entitled to success – or when they view smaller clubs as being necessary only in their defined role as losers, rather than as the intrinsically valuable expression of the hopes and efforts of a group of people.

But they are never more wrong than when they confuse glory with money.

Because every club should be selfish for glory. It is fleeting and majestic and must be hard-won and enjoyed deliriously. It's yours and your fans' alone.

The money, though, that's everyone's and winning gives you no rights to it.

15.

'I'm going to crush you on here because I'm tired of hearing about it.'

Because the truth isn't off limits.

IN his essay, 'Sport and the English Language', George Orwell wrote of the depressing sight of television presenters endlessly mouthing clichés like 'fiercely contested', 'questionable decision', 'late consolation', 'sensational performance'. Trafficking in such thoughtless, empty language has a dehumanising effect on both the speaker and his audience, dulling their brains and tending to produce unquestioning acquiescence to the status quo.

And this, don't forget, was April 1946 – a full six months before the BBC broadcast the first coverage of a football match on British TV. Michael Owen wouldn't be born for another 33 years.

Orwell, a fanatical supporter of Barcelona, in whose honour he would later pen *A Homage to Catalonia*, detailing the long-running conflict between the communally owned *Blaugrana* and the Franco-supported Real Madrid, was deeply concerned by the capacity of language to mislead and, eventually, to distort the thoughts not just of the audience but its speaker.

Football is becoming one of the more dishonest sports in the world. Not just because of the corrupt people who govern it[25] or the crooks who own the clubs, but because, among the global sports, none has made the public expression of truth so uncommon as to create a culture of obliviousness to it.

And here I don't mean Arsene Wenger's lifelong struggle with intermittent myopia or Dalglish's stirring t-shirt-based defence of racism. Wenger is one of the more thoughtful managers in the game and Dalglish is an unapologetic Liverpool partisan. No, this goes beyond any awkward post-match dissembling and Anfield fundamentalism, and touches instead on agenda control.

Simply put, football is unable and unwilling to address anything that might matter to its fans. Unconsciously or otherwise, statements by players, managers

'New Field' named, after a public vote, in honour of Orwell, using his preferred plain Spanish.

and administrators no longer have any communicative purpose other than to fill column inches and news bulletins in the least controversial manner possible.

This is the extreme corporate end of public relations, where a strategy of maintaining a perpetually burnished, family friendly image collapses into what the American philosopher Harry Frankfurt termed simply 'bullshit'. That is, saying whatever it takes to get your way without worrying if it's true or false or if it contradicts something you've previously said.[26]

Politicians are, of course, the master practitioners of such self-serving discourse. And for obvious reasons: their entire careers are spent in a death-trap dungeon, where the slightest misstep can result in a painful ending. Even an election victory simply postpones the moment when they are thrust again into the trial of champions. 'All political lives, unless they are cut off in midstream at a happy juncture, end in failure,' wrote Enoch Powell, who lived to be 85.

The Premier League would seem to present fewer opportunities for career suicide. Football players are, for example, far more likely than politicians to be judged on their actual performance, rather than their appearance. Nevertheless, a pronounced indifference to anything other than playing the game and getting paid has been present in the game for so long that it seems never to occur to players that there is such a thing as the truth, and that it might need either concealing or broadcasting.

And yet it was reported last year that Newcastle were mooting charging the media for access to their players.[27] Even by the standards of a club that employed Joe Kinnear twice, this is a remarkable plan. Will anyone, even a tabloid hack, want to pay for the thoughts of a Premier League player? Well, perhaps they'd like privileged access to the reckons of Tim Krul, whose fascinatingly banal Twitter stream includes posts like:

@TimKrul
What a win that is .. 41 years last time we won at old Trafford.. Great spirit and believe again.. Nice journey home[28]

There's something delightfully Alan Bennettish about the bathos of triumphing at the Theatre of Dreams for the first time in over four decades… and then having a pleasant coach ride home.

'Anyone who holds with the idea of free will, if considered as traditionally resting on the principle of alternative possibilities, should, in my view, stick it up their bollocks.'

@TimKrul
Nice waking up with 3 points in the bag.. Now looking forward in meeting up again with the Dutch team tomorrow..[29]

There's also something likeably innocent about the idea that the thrill of victory is so spellbinding that even a good night's sleep won't diminish it. Given how miserable many Dutch internationals have historically appeared when on duty, Krul's wide-eyed simpleness could be just the tonic.

And if those messages don't have you reaching for your wallet, perhaps you'd like to pay for first dibs on the thoughts of captain Steven Taylor? He doesn't just send comically racist tweets, you know. He has a blog too.

A typical entry might include his thoughts on defeating Spurs. Thoughts like, 'Ok yes, they had chances, but in the Premier League you can have as many chances as you like but if you don't take it, it will cost you and it has cost spurs yesterday.'[30]

At this point, I'm a bit stuck. I don't want to quote just one post, lest it appear I'm cherry-picking. But I doubt anyone could sit through even half of any given entry on the blog.

One more quote, then, for a report on playing Southampton, 'From the fans point of view I think it was a great game to watch as both sides played good football and create chances. At half time the lads wanted to keep them under pressure.'[31]

Ah! Enough!

As well as making a strong pitch to replace Alan Hansen on *Match of the Day*, Taylor's blog revealed the truth about footballers: by birth or by training, they are remarkably bland. And, in an era when we want to be ever closer to the action – inside not just the dressing room but the players' heads – English football can't oblige us, leaving the 24-hour news cycle pedalling furiously on flat tyres.[43]

While football pundits have an almost complete inability to say anything interesting about the game, they can at least tiptoe up to the uncrossable invisible line and lightly criticise a player. Admittedly, it's usually only for things that are quite hard to defend – like punching an opponent, going on strike or making anti-Semitic gestures. Actually dissecting a player's physical and mental skillset and highlighting deficiencies is the other side of the line.

The pundits, though, by virtue of no longer playing and hence not being in a position to breach the sanctity of the changing room, seem bound by a less stringent version of Football's Official Secrets Act than do the players. Serving pros maintain a level of studied opacity that the NSA will be looking to introduce to all post-Snowden recruits. Here is a group of people who would struggle with the vocabulary in a Harry Potter story but are able, to a man, to get through a press conference without ever expressing an opinion, revealing any information not already in the public domain or criticising a fellow pro. If only the ECB had access to bats this straight.

There is a general assumption that, if you don't work in a job, you aren't equipped to talk knowledgably about it. Alan Hansen, a keen early-Wittgensteinian, once invoked it with ludicrous and affronted hauteur to silence Colin Murray, setting off a career death spiral for the likeable Ulsterman. In football, it seems, the crime of speaking honestly is banishment to talkSPORT, a radio station that was, ironically, the brainchild of fearless defender of the truth Kelvin MacKenzie.

On the face of it, though, the claim to privileged knowledge isn't unreasonable. Doubtless there is a great deal to football that is mysterious to the outsider.

What seems harder to defend is the subsequent refusal to actually share that insider knowledge. Notably, the only significant and interesting voice to emerge from a still active pro felt the need to write under a nom de plume. The Secret Footballer, widely supposed to be Dave Kitson, is the first working player to really take us inside the dressing room and help us understand the world of the people we idolise. As a former Reading fan, I wouldn't be at all surprised if it was Kitson. Even at the relative height of his powers he was always a man

---

43 In the summer of 2014, Russell Wilson, who won the Super Bowl in his second season as a player, penned an essay for an American sports website about race and the NFL. He produced 2,000 coherent, thoughtful words on the notion that the most remarkable thing about him being a Super Bowl winning quarterback was that no one mentioned he was black. This, he said, rightly, was a significant marker of progress because, until the last 20 years, black quarterbacks were comparatively rare – there being an old and unspoken assumption in the game that it was a 'white' position. It would be like a young black footballer reflecting on the progress inherent in it being unremarkable to have a black captain of the English football team. The key take out for me, though, was: we should send all football players to university. When, I wondered, was the last time a football player (Frank Lampard aside, of course) wrote an essay other than in detention and on a subject other than 'Why I must not carve "Gazza is God" into the desks with the point of my compass'?

apart; a fascinating mixture of brains and self-doubt, keenly aware that football is ridiculous but determined to make it his way to a better life. Like Roy Keane, but with A Levels and well-thought opinions rather than barely-suppressed rage, Kitson learned early in his Reading career that a thoughtful, articulate man will always be an outsider in the moron bowl of professional football. After repeatedly being the subject of abuse over his red hair, Kitson complained that he was expected to suffer taunts that were akin to racism.

'If a black guy goes out there and 25,000 chant at him "you black this" or "you black that" I don't see what the difference is if you replace it with a colour of hair or anything else,' he said. 'I'm pretty sure it's this thing that people think they can come in, pay their money and shout whatever they like as their release – the English mentality is that that's acceptable. And quite frankly it isn't.

'I don't think being paid thousands of pounds a week has any bearing on whether someone can call you a black this or a ginger that or anything else to be perfectly honest. This is not how human beings behave – certainly not the way I was brought up.

'You put on a brave face on the pitch, but sometimes you can come off the pitch feeling so empty especially if you've lost and you've taken a lot of stick, and it just amazes me how no one has ever addressed it before.' [32]

He shouldn't have been amazed. Gordon Taylor, English football's sinecured answer to Sepp Blatter, quickly weighed in on the side of one of his members.[44] Or rather he didn't because this wasn't an issue that either (1) affected a current England international or (2) had any mileage with sponsors.

'It belittles racism to compare the two issues,' he said. 'It is just an opportunity for someone to have a go in same way as if you are bald or fat. Dave should be proud of his hair. It makes him stand out if he is having a good game and he could always dye it if he wants.'

At least Sepp Blatter could try and excuse his drunk-uncle ineptness by pointing out English isn't his first language. Given his thoughtless dismissal by Taylor, no wonder Kitson decided that anything he had to say in future might be better said pseudonymously.

Of course, in the Premier League, under no circumstances is it permissible for a player or manager to criticise the technique or ability of his own players or team-mates. And, only under rare circumstances – usually only the performance of a spectacular foul – may a manager comment on another team's player. In this case, the appropriate method is a pursed-lipped denunciation.

Anything more, the authorities hint darkly, risks an immediate return to the heyday of the Chelsea Headhunters, something that wouldn't be conducive to football's family friendly image.

Other iron laws governing post-game communication include:

---

44 Gordon Taylor has been chief executive of the PFA since 1981 – 33 years in the post. No wonder, then, that the attitudes of the organisation can on occasions seem a little stale. Anyone who doubts the merits of term limits should Google a list of heads of state who've been in power for more than 20 years.

Gordon Taylor, 'Red or black? No, it's green you've got to watch for, Dave.'

- A manager may, from time to time, condemn the performance of his team, but never an individual within it.
- If a player makes a terrible mistake – an attacking player misses a clear goalscoring opportunity, for example, or a goalkeeper allows the ball through his hands and into the net – before any criticism is levelled, a manager must first lightly excuse the player, prefacing his remarks with something like, 'I thought he had a good game today,' only then noting that '[the player] will be disappointed with that one'.
- If a player commits an egregious foul and no possible error by the referee can be found to divert attention, then a manager may state, 'He should know better than that.'
- On the rare occasions that a commentator fails to refrain from critiquing the workplace performance of an employee paid millions of pounds a year and offers more than a mild rebuke, players may respond to such criticisms by noting only that '[the commentator] is entitled to his opinion'.

And it continues. Football, a sport whose numbers are continually replenished by teenagers who've had their key academic years taken from them, has a prevailing culture where one must never express any honest opinion for fear of 'bringing the game into disrepute'.

Few have done more than Joey Barton to harm the reputation of the game, but, for all his messianic delusions, he's still the man most likely to break the code. Few things he's said, even the quotes from Nietzsche, have the cut-through of his put-down to England players promoting their quadrennial autobiographies, 'I went to the World Cup, we were shit, buy my book – who wants to read that?' Orwell would've shuffled uncomfortably in the face of such confident working class self-expression but later penned an essay commending the earthy Anglo-Saxonness of it.

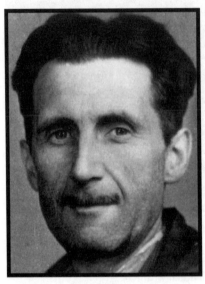

'Shit ground, no fans.'[45]

Like politics, where, out of a belief that one must never be caught changing one's mind or disagreeing with a colleague, its professional practitioners take pains never to be caught saying anything concrete, it's unthinkable that a manager or player would say anything as simple and straightforward as, 'He played very badly today. He missed important passes when it counted. He needs to prepare better and work harder.'

Contrast this with the NFL, where – far from allowing clubs to charge for their time – players are *required* to be available for the media four days a week.

This massive, compulsory media exposure inevitably draws out a huge quantity of non-news, clichés, studied blandness and third-person self-praise from players, pundits and coaches alike. But it also engenders a great deal of what, to the British eye, seems surprising and refreshingly honest critical appraisals of players, often from their own team-mates.

Last season, when Washington's quarterback, Robert Griffin III, was struggling after a return from injury, he gave a post-match interview where he questioned the head coach's game plan and denied responsibility for a badly thrown pass that was intercepted, saying, 'Nobody got open.'

---

45 For more on Orwell's personal experience of the scandalous conditions then prevailing in lower league football in the north of England, I recommend *The Road to Wigan Athletic*.

With the media abuzz with rumours of locker-room dissatisfaction about the still-young Griffin's attitude, veteran wide receiver Santana Moss defended his coach, saying, 'To be honest with you, [the coach's] far from [having] lost us. What he says, we listen loud and clear. When it comes down to coaching the team, I think he's one of the best that's done it. I've been around a lot of coaches and he prepares us well.'

Then, turning his attention to Griffin's failure to take responsibility for his mistakes, he said, 'As a leader, you understand that if you're involved in the situation, whether you're the receiver, the quarterback, the guys making the tackle, whoever, regardless of the outcome, good or bad, you have to at some point, stand up and say "me" or "I". If we're going to win games, we need to win games with our guy saying, "At the end of the day, I didn't make a play."'

Imagine how different Nicklas Bendtner's career could have been if he'd been put in his place like this five years ago.

Occasionally, this kind of day-to-day banter explodes and takes in bigger issues. And, because the NFL is a sport played by men who've not been completely robbed of an education, when it does, the results can be spectacular.

In 2011, when the NFL and the players' association were trying to finalise an agreement on pay, conditions, player safety and other issues, it was reported that several senior players had requested special exemptions from some of the regulation. Chris Kluwe, Minnesota's punter, criticised the players for being greedy, only to find himself on the subject of an article by former Denver player Nate Jackson, called, 'When We Want The Punter's Opinion, We'll Ask For It (We Won't)'. It included some pretty salty words of disrespect for punters – players often caricatured as even more oddball than football's goalkeepers. Kluwe, he said, was a turncoat who'd failed to understand the negotiation procedure. Worse, the peripheral role of punters on teams – isolated individuals, he said, who'd be the first to be eaten if a plane crash on a desert island necessitated cannibalism – meant that Kluwe hadn't any legitimate right to present himself as a leader of or spokesman for the players.[33]

The next day, Kluwe responded with some invective of his own, challenging Jackson's right to silence him. It was ridiculous, Kluwe said, to argue publically that, in effect, only star players should be allowed to comment on the negotiations when Jackson himself had had such a negligible career. Kluwe restated that he'd continue to speak out when he perceived players, no matter how famous, were behaving like 'grasping, blackmailing, money-grubbing jerks' and reminded Jackson how crucial it was to the future of the sport that fans believed that players recognised how privileged they were.32 All in all, it was a delicious dustup.[34]

Now imagine what would happen if you asked Steven Gerrard and Rio Ferdinand to debate, in an exchange of letters, say, the rights and wrongs of Qatar 2022. Of course, you'd be asking the wrong people; Frank Lampard is the clever one, they say. Clever enough, certainly, to get a five-book publishing deal for his children's stories. And yet, when asked by *The Guardian* if he'd actually written the first book, he responded, 'Yeah, bits of it… I would love to get to the stage where I can actually write the whole book myself.'

'Eh, 'ow do you spell "the scandal of indentured labour"?'

Of course, not all player NFL commentary contains shattering insights or public dressings-down. Nor is speech completely free (Chris Kluwe would later leave the game claiming his outspoken manner, particularly his support for equal marriage, made teams unwilling to sign him).

What there is, though, is no conspiracy of silence, no self-censorship. A fan can engage with the sport knowing that the issues they care about will be discussed, however badly.

And, even if the subject isn't always lofty, the eloquence and showmanship of some players overflows into glorious trash-talking. You may have seen Richard Sherman's extraordinary post-game verbal assault on an opponent after the 2013/14 NFC Championship game. (YouTube 'Richard Sherman' and 'Michael Crabtree'.) What's delightful about Sherman is that it barely makes it into his top 30 interviews.

In 2013, he was a guest on a TV show with Skip Bayless, a polarising figure in US sports who'd previously criticised Sherman's claims to be the best at his position despite being just two years into his career.

In a defiant, dismissive and wonderfully mental take-down of the NFL's answer to Steve Claridge, Sherman exploded, 'Whenever you refer to me, whenever you speak to me, whenever you address me, address me as All-Pro, Stanford graduate – because those are some accomplishments you will aspire to but never accomplish. You have never accomplished anything.'

When Bayless responded, talking up his own achievements, Sherman continued, 'I'm All-Pro. I'm one of the best 22 players in the NFL. You're going to brush it off, but I don't think you're the best 22 anything.'

A helpless Bayless replied, 'Now you wanna trash talk me, which is totally cool with me,' before Sherman finished him off with, 'I'm intelligent enough and

'Tell Frank Lampard that 11 GCSEs won't even get you an interview at Stanford.'

capable enough to understand that you are an ignorant, pompous, egotistical, cretin. I'm going to crush you on here because I'm tired of hearing about it.'

Some people have seen Richard Sherman play and heard him speak and yet don't like him. I find this amazing. To me, he's one of the few sportsman in recent years who can actually talk the talk like Muhammad Ali. Who cares that he's brash and over-the-top? When you've been through what Sherman (and every other player) has to reach the pro game, when you've sacrificed and dedicated yourself to a sport in a way that most football players could never conceive of, when you've taken the endless verbal kickings that the US sports media deals out, then damn it, you're entitled to a little swagger.

Contrast this with the silent, sulking reserve of most English players, who channel their distrust and detestation of the British public into a biennial subconscious summer go-slow.

It's understandable, of course, that not everyone wants to unpin a career hand grenade every week. But if you come to find that speaking plainly is a barely practised skill; something, in fact, to be avoided professionally, then, at that point, you've begun to hold the public in contempt.

And there lies the problem. Secrecy breeds not just dangerous isolation for our sporting and political classes, but corruption too. Football is no more the people's sport than politicians are the people's representatives. We are an inconvenience and an embarrassment to them; formerly part-owners, now customers to be milked and bilked.

In the NFL – for all the vacuum pull of money, which draws out convenient deception like puss from a wound – there are enough inherited traditions and enforced rules to demonstrate, if not a total commitment to truth, then a collective recognition that openness is vital to keeping the game honest.

Take attitudes to money, for example. As part of the salary cap, the length and value of all players' contracts are in the public domain. Likewise, each week every team must publish their injury report, detailing the health status of any player not deemed to be 100 per cent. No Hoddle-esque pretending a player was injured when he wasn't.

Ultimately, does it *matter* that the Premier League is the home of the 'undisclosed fee' and the 'signed for a reported £X,000 a week' story? I think it does, because it is this lacuna that creates an ecological niche for agents, gamblers and skimming-administrators to thrive.

In other words, the stringent efforts that football makes to ensure the continuing banality of all reporting on the game isn't a minor presentational issue. It's indicative of a deep-seated contempt for the public that's taken hold in a game now completely removed from its former unofficial collective public ownership.

When an institution is no longer transparent or accountable to the people in whose interests it was created, when an entryist faction has infiltrated that institution and made change from within impossible, then, whether it is the footballing or political authorities – the graft-stained corridors of FIFA, the Premier League reputation laundering factory or the benches of the House of Commons, green with lobbyist cash – that institution is no longer legitimate and must be replaced.

16.

'I just gave it a try and it went out in a special way.'

Because the big game never gets spoiled by negativity.

ARLIER this month all the worms in my garden died on the same day. The cause of death wasn't pesticides or eagle-eyed early birds. It was drowning.

I was at home, working at the kitchen table. Outside, yet another of the winter's endless downpours was bouncing off the patio. Looking up, I saw a writhing tangle of pink spaghetti emerging from the grass, which was finally uninhabitably saturated. The worms struggled desperately on to the slabs, searching in vain for high ground, only to expire in the shallow puddles outside my French windows.

It was a terrible thing, wormageddon. And yet it was still a less abject sight than Denver in that week's Super Bowl.[46]

Rising from my chair, and without even thinking to becoat myself, I stepped outside, scooping up the inanimate invertebrates and flinging them over the wall into next door's garden, lest they disturb my children on their return from nursery (don't worry, I threw them in three batches in three different places to avoid arousing the suspicion of my neighbours).

---

46 In case you missed it, the score was 43–8, with Seattle's first points coming after just 12 seconds following a horrible mistake by Denver on the first play of the game. Denver didn't get on the scoreboard until the end of the third quarter, by which time they were already 36 points down. The game was over long before that, though. Seattle went in at half-time 22–0 up, which is a commanding lead, but much of the half-time chat was spent discussing how Denver could get back into it. The expectation was they would emerge from the dressing room, score early and then apply pressure to Seattle. In fact, however, Seattle returned the opening kick-off of the second half for a touchdown, killing the game stone dead.

The Denver offence goes three-and-out again.[47]

The whole thing took about 30 seconds. Just slightly longer than it took for Seattle to begin disposing of Peyton Manning's wretched offensive.

The 2013/14 Super Bowl was the worst I've seen in years. Horrendously one-sided, epically anticlimatic and without a single momentum shift or wrinkle to give it colour. If most Super Bowls are symphonies, this was a bad punk single: three chords – Seattle D# Denver O□ (Manning diminished), Seattle O, repeat.

With Denver fielding what was, statistically, the greatest single-season offence off all time and Seattle rolling out a league-best defensive unit, expectations were high for an archetypical unstoppable-force-versus-immoveable-object clash. And, as it's supposed to, the unstoppable force stopped and the immoveable object moved. Except the direction the immoveable object moved wasn't away from the unstoppable force, but downfield, towards the Denver endzone, with the ball, on yet another interception return.

It was as if a game had been arranged between the Arsenal Invincibles of 2003/04 and the Bould- and Adams-led stonewall of 1998/99. But, instead of the obvious outcomes – another 1-0 to the Arsenal or an Henry and Vieira masterclass – the George Graham holdovers had somehow thrashed the pass-and-move maestros 5-0.

---

47 'The rain came down hard that night and washed the paint clean off the cars. We slept in the basement for shelter, emerging to see the denuded metalwork a reticent, sickly grey in the morning light, like a scalp freshly shaved for a do-or-die procedure. No birds sang.'

Peyton Manning gears up for another shot at the Seattle defence.

It wasn't just that English football's greatest ever backline had neutralised and then brutalised Wenger's magnus opus. Nor was it that tempo, precision and athleticism had failed to exhaust and torment the acme of the English 4-4-2. Rather, it was as though, to a man, Bergkamp, Pires, Ljungberg, Cole, Campbell, Lauren, Toure, Gilberto, Lehmann, Henry and Vieira had all failed to show.

And yet, for all this, this year's Super Bowl was still better than half the World Cup or European Championship finals played in my lifetime. And for one very simple reason: in the NFL there is no tactical trade-off between a strong defence and an aggressive, creative offence.

An NFL defence can be every bit as disciplined, efficient and ruthless as a football one, but never at the expense of their attacking options or the overall quality of the game.

When a team loses the ball (provided an interception isn't returned for a touchdown), there's a pause and 11 offensive players are replaced with 11 defenders. This means an NFL coach never has to ask himself, 'Is it an extra linebacker or another wide receiver I need?'

Provided they stay within the salary cap, then, teams' ability to excel at offence *and* defence is circumscribed only by how well they draft, develop and coach players.

So, while you can admire and adore a tough centre-back or a flying left-back, it is only in the NFL that defences can produce players who are the equal of offences; players who can be glorious and ugly, creative and brutal in equal measure. Defending in the NFL is something that can be enjoyed as a populist pastime, not in the masochistic, monastic or snobbish way of those

Defending in the NFL and the Premier League.

who profess to prefer a well-organised back four to a free-flowing possession-hungry midfield.

As a result, the answer to the question 'When was the last time a Super Bowl was ruined by a negative coach?' is, 'Not in my lifetime'. The same cannot be said for the finals of the major football competitions.

Only two of the eight World Cup finals I've seen have actually been really good games; ones of appreciable skill, fluidity, precision and verve. Five of the six that weren't good were actually dreadful, with Holland (2010), Italy (2006 and 1994) and Argentina (1990) determining successfully to spoil the game.

When executed correctly, the kung-fu kick need not always spoil a game.

The 2014 World Cup final was a decent-ish game illuminated by a lovely goal at the death (how close we were to yet another final decided by penalties).[48]

It's notable that the most interesting moments of the previous two World Cup finals were acts of violence: Zidane's glorious headbutt and de Jong's shameful karate kick. In other words, the only truly memorable events in these sporting perihelia were essentially non-footballing actions.

The best final of my lifetime was Argentina's 3-2 win against Germany in 1986 – which also happens to be from my favourite World Cup of all time. But then perhaps being nine is the best time to enjoy football.

The Euro finals don't fare much better. Three of the last seven have been good, with two – 1992 and 1988 – being classics. And, while you wouldn't exactly call 1992 a technically great game, it was one of football's most abiding underdog stories (when Greece triumphed against the odds 12 years later it was a much less appealing spectacle, which tells us, at least, that you can win matches by parking buses, but to win hearts you must get off the bus and run around a bit).

The 1988 encounter was a much more clear-cut classic, not least because it featured what I hold to be the greatest goal in an international final. Go and relive it now. Go on, treat yourself.

Watching Marco van Basten's volley again it's unnerving how long the ball is in the air; it just won't come down. And then, when it does, his otherworldly body control defies belief. Put it on again and, this time, ignore the ball and stay with van Basten. He lands perfectly in-stride and on-balance after striking the ball. The grainy nature of the film and the uncanny slowness of it all makes you wonder if you've accidentally clicked on a Pro Evolution Soccer re-enactment of the moment.

Talking about the goal later, van Basten admitted that his volley had been prompted more by tiredness than anything else – he simply didn't think he had enough left in the tank to bring the ball down and drive at the defender. So, with charming modesty and understatement, he 'just gave it a try and it went out in a special way in the goal'.

Goal-wise, major football finals have tended to produce slim pickings. Prior to 2014, seven of the last 14 teams to contest a World Cup Final had scored in normal time. The average score after 90 minutes was 1.57-0.43. Likewise, five of the last 14 teams to play in a Euro final haven't scored in normal time, giving an average 90-minute score of 1.71-0.29.

If that seems a bit abstract, the average score in the 380 Premier League games in 2012/13 was 2.02-0.78 – about 0.4 of an extra goal for both winning and losing teams. So, while the margin of victory is typically similar, big competition finals produce fewer goals that a standard Premier League game. Over the last 26 years, a World Cup or Euro final has seen the winning team score 19 per cent fewer goals than a Premier League match while the loser scored 54 per cent fewer goals.

---

48 The tournament itself was marvellous. Goals, surprises, atmosphere. About the only way you could improve on the 2014 World Cup would be to play it in slave-built compounds in 50°C desert heat.

Now, while final score is no measure of the quality of a football game, I don't think it's unfair to use it as an indicator of its openness. Compared to the NFL, football's big occasions don't measure up so well. Seattle's 35-point margin of victory was two more points than the combined margin of victory for the winning teams in the previous six Super Bowls.

In fact, the last nine Super Bowls before 2013/14 have been won by an average margin of 6.56 points – less than a touchdown and an extra point.

The last time a team lost a Super Bowl by more than 14 points (two TDs with extra points), was 2002/03 when the Raiders got a 48-21 spanking. And the last time before Denver that a team scored fewer than 14 points in a Super Bowl was Seattle's 21-10 defeat by Pittsburgh in the 2005/06 season.

Meanwhile, the average score from the last ten Super Bowls (this year's included) has been 27.4-18. The average score in the 256 regular season games in 2013/14 was 28.8-17.7, which means recent Super Bowls (including 2013/14's blow-out) have seen winning teams scoring just 4.8 per cent fewer points than in the regular season while the losing team actually scored 1.6 per cent more points than in the regular season.

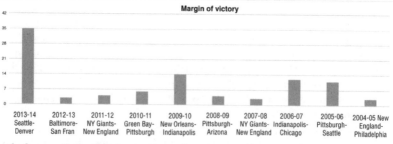

The last ten Super Bowl points spreads.

How football and the NFL perform on the big occasions.[49]

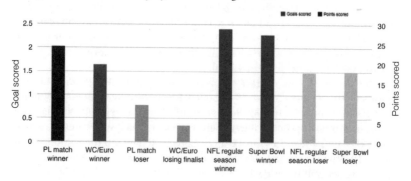

49 Averages taken from last 7 World Cup and Euro finals (at 90 mins), all 2012/13 Premier League final scores, last 10 Super Bowls and all 2013 NFL regular season games in (excluding overtime).

What does all this redundant precision tell us? That Super Bowls tend to be played with an openness and offensive intent (as measured by the score and points spread) that pretty closely resembles any NFL normal fixture, while international football tournament finals are cagey, low-scoring affairs, lacking the flair of a top flight game in one of Europe's better leagues. Put simply, in the Super Bowl, nerves or tactics don't get the better of the occasion.

If this, or any other of my criticisms of football as we know it today – wages, concentration of talent, quality of administration, for example – doesn't sound all that remarkable, I put it to you that this is not because it's not important, but just that, as football fans, we've got quite used to simply taking what we are given by the game, without any hope of improvement. The moment everyone believes nothing can be done, they're right.

Another measure of quality, albeit more subjective, is memorability. I recall only one thing from the last World Cup Final – the goal – and only four from the 2010 one: the foul and attendant outrage, a deep distaste for van Bommel, Fernando Torres's broken lumbering and Iniesta's limp winner.

Compare that with my favourite recent Super Bowl: Super Bowl XLIII in early 2009. Held in Tampa, it began with Jennifer Hudson singing the national anthem before a squadron of Top Gun F16s did a flypast. Then, appearing on the pitch only two weeks after they shot to world attention for their astonishing landing of a plane on the Hudson River was the crew of US Airways Flight 1549, led by the endearing Captain Chesley B. Sullenberger. They took the applause of the crowd before the coin toss ceremony, a ceremony itself that was performed by General David Petraeus, formerly the most senior American soldier in Iraq, later the sexually incontinent director of the CIA. All this happened before a single second of play had elapsed. At half-time Bruce Springsteen did a medley of his greatest hits.

Granted, those are non-sporting memories, but it does go to show that World Cup finals have an ineffable greyness to them. It's always mildly surprising how little imagination appears to go into their staging.

In the game itself, there were numerous remarkable events, not least the sight of James Harrison, a 17-stone meathead with enough rage to scare a 'roid dealer, intercepting the ball in his own endzone. This supreme power machine, built for short sprints and fearsome upper body strength, raced 106 yards to the other endzone before being felled at the goal line and having to receive oxygen on the sideline. It was literally a lung-busting run.

Later in the game, down 20–7 going into the final quarter, Arizona, led by quarterback Kurt Warner, rallied remarkably and edged into a three-point lead with just minutes to play. Warner, whose career is a wonderful story in its own right, was in his penultimate season. His three touchdowns and 377 yards cemented his place not just as one of the game's great quarterbacks but one of the very best on the big stage.

And yet, despite his brilliance, it was not to be. Pittsburgh went right back down the other end and their quarterback, the mercurial Ben Roethlisberger, threw a pass which looked to be going out, but was somehow hauled in by Santonio Holmes. It was a van Basten-esque moment of skill, capping off a game that really did have everything.

Several other recent Super Bowls have been decided on literally the last play of the game, with the advantage swinging repeatedly in the final quarter of the game. If only football's big games could say the same.

Were previous finals before 1988 any better? I don't know. I haven't watched them, though match reports suggest not.

Football, it seems, is a sport frequently overwhelmed by its own occasions.

There's an argument that knockout football isn't really football at all. The game really only makes sense as a league, where enough games are played to iron out the element of randomness in a game where scoring is so difficult. Leagues, of course, are anticlimactic in a different way: the winner is usually decided several games before the end, creating a series of dead rubbers.

And that's the flaw in big football matches: with individual games so hard to win and defending in numbers having so often proved to be the best strategy for weaker teams, it becomes impossible to ensure open and attractive games.

It's a big problem and one that won't be solved by arguing about extra time, replays, golden goals or penalties. Big games will continue to make negative tactics likely until something fundamental changes.

Like what? Well, how about, for example: bigger goals?

The current goal height (2.44m) and width (7.33m) of goals has remained unchanged since the 1880s. This gives an area of 17.86m^2 in which to score.

According to the BBC, the average UK man in the 1870s was 1.67m high. Figures for 2010 show the average UK man is now 1.77m high – ten centimetres taller.[35]

The world's first goalpost in Sheffield, England. Brian Deane missed his first open goal here in 1882.

Relative to player height, then, goals have shrunk by over 11 per cent. Scale up a goal to the proportions of a modern day player and the posts would be 44cm further apart and 15cm higher. With an area of 20.10m^2, strikers would have 12.5 per cent more target to hit. For a player lining up a shot, that's basically increasing the goal by an extra ball's width at each side of the keeper and raising the bar by three-quarters of a ball.

In simple terms, almost every shot you've ever seen hit the post or bar would've gone in.

Even then, you could argue, coaches would adapt. As shots would be more likely to go in the catenaccio would return, with players instructed to close down even tighter and prevent shots. You might find, though, that the increase in fouling this would bring would create more free kicks near goal, which would be even more valuable than they are now. The game could become a stalemate, decided by the quality of free-kick taking rather than open play.

With ever more riding on the outcome of football's big games, it's hard to see what measures could be taken to prevent the sport's future showpiece occasions being huge disappointments.

Football, like tennis, is a game that sometimes seems like it's running low on options. Woven into its very design are a set of assumptions about human physical limits that are centuries out of date. Players now are too big, too strong, too quick, too well coached, too tactically aware and too well rewarded for finals to be meaningful affairs.

Change will require considerable tinkering with the rules and playing space – unlimited substitutions; the return of subbed-off players; a bigger pitch; one fewer outfielders – and the outcome may be something far different to the game we know now.[50][36] Either that or we stop pretending that football will deliver on the big occasions and consider dropping the knockout element of the final stages.

The Super Bowl, meanwhile, no matter how big it grows, will always be able to make you this promise: one team can fail to show, but a team can never spoil it by playing negatively.

---

50 Kirk Goldsberry, writing for the ever wonderful *Grantland*, did have one beguilingly simple suggestion: move the penalty spot further away from the goal. In World Cups, he said, penalties were converted at a rate of 81 per cent, making them overwhelmingly worth playing (and diving) for. Experiment, he suggested, in moving the penalty spot back far enough that the likelihood of scoring is dramatically reduced – to, say, 50 per cent or 33 per cent. It's telling, I think, that this elegant, measurable idea for reform comes from an American writer drawing on his knowledge of basketball. His use of statistics is also brilliant. We tend to criticise players most for going down if we feel they could've stayed up and got a clean shot away, especially in a one-on-one situation. But in so doing we dramatically overestimate how easy scoring is. In the piece, Goldsberry juxtaposed the conversion percentage on penalties with the conversion rate for shots in the group stages of the 2014 World Cup. Quoting Opta, he said, 'Even within five yards of the goal, players still fail to convert even half of their shots.' Is it any wonder, then, that winning or avoiding penalties so dominates the thinking of players and managers?

17.

'I'm going all in with Andy Impey.'
Because there's stability of ownership.

NOSTALGIA is a form of psychic defence mechanism: the inexorable attachment to the mistaken belief that things in the past were better gives us mental shelter from the awfulness of the present. Thanks to the internet – where all new technologies are pioneered by pornography, popularised by hipsters and then polluted with presenile reminiscence by the middle-aged public – nostalgia is better than it's ever been. For football fans, in whom nostalgia rises to the level of a mental disorder, it's doubly so.

And thank God, because without it I'd have to care about Alan Pardew nearly headbutting someone. I'd have to have an opinion about the remarkable success of the Southampton youth academy. I'd have to give *real* thought to Demba Ba. And why would I want to do that when I could be thinking about Ian Culverhouse?

I've spent enough of my life in pubs talking about football that they ought to qualify as a place of work on my CV. And yet I'd never heard of the Ian Culverhouse game until *Guardian* journalist Barry Glendenning tweeted this:

> @bglendenning
> @maxrushden Lets get long-running game of 'Ian Culverhouse' going on twitter. Takes just one spoilsport: Ian Bishop #ianculverhouse[37]

For people of a certain age, nothing else need be said. To know who Ian Culverhouse is is to immediately know we're playing a word association game that involves naming footballing journeymen of the early 1990s. Even the choice of player – Norwich's dependable right-back – is so obviously correct as to need no explanation; no one has ever argued that he was a massively underrated talent who, but for Gary Stevens and Lee Dixon, would've been capped many times by his country. He was the epitome of memorably pleasant mediocrity from an era when grounds were tin-roofed toilets, pitches were bomb sites and players appeared to be only slightly better that you might have been had you had access to some better coaching at school.

Unlike musical nostalgia, which tells you that music died when you were 18 and that nothing can ever sound as good again, footballing nostalgia tends to a perverse celebration of the reassuring stability of the unremarkable. The not famous, the not brilliant, the solid, the triers and the underachievers, the not quite rubbish.

The early 1990s was a golden age of averageness with a special flag-bearer called Norwich City. The game is named after Ian Culverhouse, but it could just have easily been any of his team-mates: Goss, Crook, Bowen or any of the defence that, with Culverhouse, made the Canaries' team sheet read like a business card from Norfolk's leading firm of solicitors: Ullathorne, Butterworth and Polston.

If this sounds like a dig at Culverhouse or his contemporaries, it's really not meant to be. With every response to Glendenning's tweet, the wonderful memories came rushing back.

> @bglendenning
> yes, nice. "@danjkahn: @bglendenning Jason Dozzell #ianculverhouse"[38]

> @bglendenning
> a personal favourite "@mholforduk: @bglendenning Steve Vickers #ianculverhouse"[39]

> @bglendenning
> Love how many people just 'get' the @maxrushden '#ianculverhouse' game and – incredibly – @jonawils is still winning #ericyoung[40]

> @bglendenning
> perfect. this man understands "@fhugob: Chris Kiwomya? @ bglendenning #ianculverhouse"[41]

> @bglendenning
> way too good. and famous. you are out #ianculverhouse "@ MrIanStewart: @bglendenning Kevin Sheedy."[42]

I tweeted a few responses, but stopped once I saw what I regarded as a game-endingly brilliant answer:

> @hoggy_vegas
> @bglendenning I've been waiting all my life for this game. I'm going all in with Andy Impey #IanCulverhouse[43]

Gloriously foolish as it all was, after a while it started to feel like a memorial for forgotten footballers. Ian Ormondroyd, Jan Stejskal, Torben Piechnik, Steve Chettle, Nigel Jemson, Craig Hignett. All of them hardworking pros who had good careers, who are fondly, if infrequently, remembered by at least one set of fans and who never earned in a year what Wayne Rooney makes in a week.

Sadder than that was the recognition that I found it hard to imagine playing the same game 20 years from now with Hugo Rodallega or Shola Ameobi or Ben Watson or Lee Cattermole. I mean how could you? They're not people, not real ones; they're Premier League players. You can't love something to which you feel no human connection.

Football today is a business afloat on a sea of cash, dragged from its moorings and driven by trade winds far from its home port. On deck, surrounded by hangers-on and with Steven Gerrard at the decks spinning Phil Collins, players, managers, chairmen and administrators sun themselves at the pool party, unaware that, when the wind drops, they have no idea how to get home.

Such is the fate of any sport that loses its connection with solid ground.

'Put your hands in the air! But slowly, so I don't think you might be about to hit me.'

For much of the first half of the 20th century, Detroit was America's fourth largest city. In 1950 it had 1.8m people – more than one per cent of the total US population. But, by 2010, following decades of decline, its population had collapsed to 714,000. Within its city limits, an area the size of San Francisco has been abandoned.[44] I've been to San Francisco and there's a lot of it. It's the kind of massive hole usually only found behind England full-backs in important games.

No one, of course, did more to build Detroit than Henry Ford and his family. His son and one of his grandsons both ran the company, while another,

William Clay Ford, Sr, sat on the board of Ford for 57 years. Most interesting, from our perspective, is what William did in late 1963: he bought the Detroit Lions, the city's NFL team. Paying $4.5m – somewhere about $33m in today's money – he owned the team for the final 51 years of his life before he died, aged 88, in early March 2014, and his shares passed to his family.

As it turns out, for all Ford's loyal stewardship of the team, Detroit's success on the field broadly matched that of the city: continual decline with occasional flickering but unfulfilled promises of a renaissance. Despite this, last year, Forbes estimated the Lions' value at $900m – which is the kind of return on investment that would impress even the financial tweakers of the Premier League.[45] It's also exactly the same estimated value that Forbes assigned to Chelsea, a money-pit that Roman Abramovich bought in 2003 for $230m and, depending on who you ask, has since shovelled at least a further $1bn–$1.5bn into.[46] [47]

'Pour in a load of Kežman, then top it with Schürrle and seal it with Matić.'

But Chelsea, atypically for a club recently acquired by foreign owners, may argue they have succeeded under Abramovich. Money has been poured in but, notably, the club have won some things: FA Cups, Premier Leagues, a Champions League. Grudging admiration too, sometimes, but not hearts.

In the old days, football chairmen used to see generations of fans and players come and go; respectable old men opening the turnstiles for ruddy-faced young vandals and thugs in the hope some working-class communal activity might help them develop into men of character. Now it's the opposite. Impeccably behaved, well-heeled, middle-class men watch from the stands as the directors' box becomes a reputational chrysalis, cocooning very hungry oligarchs who've grown fat on the wealth of their nation and are now ready to spread their wings as respectable members of the global yacht-set.

Such as been the focus on the Big Clubs of English football that the sheer scale of ownership transfer is easy to miss. *Every single* Premier League club has changed hands at least once in the last 20 years. In March 2014, the average length of ownership was just 7.6 years. Imagine that: national institutions, with histories of 100-plus years, being got shot of faster than a first wife. Of the 20 Premier League clubs, only eight could currently be said to be owned by people with a close tie to the club or local area. And one of these wants to change his club's name to Hull Tigers.

Stability.[51]

In the Championship the picture isn't much different. Again, the average ownership period was 7.6 years, with ten clubs being owned by locals – a figure barely better than the Premier League. Of the 24 clubs, just two – Middlesbrough and Blackpool – had been owned for 20 years or more by the same person, although an honourable mention must also go to Wigan, with Dave Whelan having already clocked up 19 years in charge by then.

In other words, only seven per cent of England and Wales's 44 biggest football clubs haven't changed hands in the last 20 years.

Compare this with the NFL, where the average team has been owned for

---

51 'And David Peace wrote his book. His long, long book. Full of statistics and team sheets and player names and crowds. He wrote his book. Not in a book, but with a computer at his home in Tokyo, Japan. And in his book, David Peace's long, long book, out of the puzzling, punishing, relentless repetition something emerged. From all that numbing detail something emerged. Something strange and magnificent. Bill Shankly and post-war English football, writ large and thrillingly alive. A masterpeace.'

more than 34 years by the same person or family. Only 11 of 32 franchises (34 per cent) changed hands in the last 20 years, with ten of 32 (31 per cent) owned by the same person/family since the team's inception. And, contrary to the image of NFL teams as being the wholly-owned toys of rich men, 18 of 32 teams (56 per cent) are owned by people or families with significant local ties. Incredibly, three teams – Pittsburgh, Chicago and the New York Giants – currently have a third- or fourth-generation owner.

Continuity – as in the case of Detroit – doesn't guarantee success, but, across a whole sport it's vital. Who is there to set norms, enforce unofficial discipline and speak for the past and the future of the game if its team owners are largely absent and frequently changing? Who will be willing to suggest – or able to sell – the notion of collective, long-term thinking and investment in the future of the game?

The incredible shenanigans at Leeds over the last few years have focused attention on the much derided Fit and Proper Person Test to which owners were supposed to be subject. In fact, though, the FA, Premier League and Football League did away with that some years ago, replacing it with the Owner's and Director's Test.

This recently lowered bar means that a prospective owner needs only to have no unspent criminal convictions in a narrow class of offences and no footballing conflicts of interest (there are a few other football-specific things governing match fixing and broadcast rights, but they needn't detain us).

Crucially, the 'test' is a simple, self-certified, three-page form that takes less time to complete than a customs card at an airport.[48] It's how money-launderer Carson Yeung, unjustly convicted businessman Alisher Usmanov, disgraced former Thai prime minister Thaksin Shinawatra and others got their hands on treasured community assets.

'I'm about 6-3, short dark hair, no criminal convictions and very, very trustworthy. Promise.'

Once you've done that you're good to go. It's regulation with an almost Dennis Bergkamp-esque lightness of touch, and yet another manifestation of the pervasive political dogma that wealthy business leaders – and only wealthy business leaders – will save us, if only democratically accountable officials would abandon discredited ideas like public service.

As Matthew Stewart, author of an insider account of management consultancies, wrote, 'When Jesus is compared with a CEO, it is Jesus who is thought to gain by the comparison.'[49] This idea found its strongest footballing expression in Hull owner Assem Allam, who spoke for the frustrated toddler inside every bloated plutocrat when, on being informed that the FA might veto his proposal to change Hull's name, he said, 'No one on earth is allowed to question my business decisions, I won't allow it.' Not even Jesus, presumably.

A liar loans process of the kind that first inflated and then exploded the American housing market, almost destroying the world economy, is applied to club ownership. How soon will it be before English football goes the same way, with corruption, criminality and the boundless vanity of the wealthy destroying the Premier League? 'Not too long, I hope' is the answer I come up with quite often these days, especially if I've been playing the Ian Culverhouse game.

So what's to be done? Enquire after the sources of wealth? Licence owners? Demand proof of their good intentions and a non-refundable deposit of hundreds of millions of pounds in the event a club should be left destitute?

With defeatism now a British national sport, it all sounds impossible. But, as always, what's lacking is not a workable solution but the willingness to look for one. Nothing's impossible if responsible people apply their minds to the problem.

Take the NFL, for example, where buying is a team a great deal more complex than getting your hands on a second-hand football club. Unlike the

'I need people to vote for me? How much does that cost?'

Premier League, where you have only to find someone who will sell you a team, the NFL constitution specifically mandates that the NFL commissioner himself must investigate any potential sale and pass it fit.

Only then does the really interesting bit kick in. Article 3.5B of the NFL constitution states, 'All sales, transfers, or assignments, except a transfer referred to in Section 3.5(C) hereof, shall only become effective if 7 Article III approved by the affirmative vote of not less than three-fourths or 20, whichever is greater, of the members of the League.'[50]

In other words, having enough money to buy a team and avoid prosecution only gets you so far. You also need to persuade the commissioner and at least 24 team owners to okay you.

Imagine what it does for a sport to have a long-lasting, mutually approved set of owners. However rich and powerful they are as individuals they have no choice but to spend time together, to hear each other's point of view, to get on and to cooperate. Over time it creates, even among some of the nation's most avaricious people, a culture of custodianship. These owners also appoint and pay the commissioner from their own pocket to run the game and, every few years, they hammer out a deal with players on revenue sharing, employment rights and other administrative issues.

Compare this to English football, whose national association has all the vitality of a leukaemic dog, whose European and global administrators are staggeringly corrupt and whose Premier League is a nest of mutually distrustful, sub-Machiavellian coup plotters.

This is not to say that the NFL doesn't have its share of problem owners. Indianapolis's Jim Irsay, who's been partial to drunk-tweeting and prescription medications, is famously the troubled son of a troublesome father (his 2014 arrest for drink-driving led to the NFL suspending one of its own owners, banning him from any contact with his own team – training ground and stadium – for over a third of a season).

Meanwhile, Dallas's owner Jerry Jones could give any recent Premier League chairman, even Mohamed Al-Fayed, a lesson in egomania and eccentricity. Unlike Irsay, though, who inherited his team, Jones bought his and persuaded the other owners to have him. And why? Because while they may wonder about his brashness, they recognised he could help drive the NFL forward. His business acumen was critical in unlocking the mega-money TV deals that have transformed the game in the last few decades.

Even when you're in the NFL owners' club, you can't relax. Unlike the Premier League, with its entirely hypothetical powers to kick out clubs run by unfit owners, or UEFA with its amusingly empty threats of Champions League exclusion for those not playing fairly financially, the NFL constitution has teeth. In the 1990s, for example, the NFL forced the scandal-hit owner of San Francisco to cede control of his team for a year, before later surrendering it to his sister in 2000.

This year it seemed like it might happen again, this time to Cleveland owner Jimmy Haslam, a billionaire whose legal troubles would've impressed Nile Ranger. In 2013, only months after becoming an NFL owner, he found his service station empire placed under FBI investigation over an alleged fraud worth up to $35m. Haslam had bought the Browns from Randy Lerner, another billionaire who'd inherited the team from his father. Sick of running an unglamorous, perennially under-performing team in a run-down, unloved city, Lerner had made a fresh start at Aston Villa. Haslam's business, meanwhile, cut a deal with the FBI and no criminal charges were pressed.

'You're going to stop me playing in Europe? Oh really?'

Even allowing for the occasional rogue owner, the NFL system is far from perfect. Perhaps the biggest strike against the NFL is that it has repeatedly allowed owners to move their teams, usually for financial reasons – something for which there is no defence. And, by that I mean there should be no defence under international law, and prosecutions in The Hague should be considered for offenders.

Community groups and charities are also specifically barred from owning a club, ruling out the kind of ownership model many older football fans dream of. Green Bay – the Barcelona of the NFL – are the only collectively-owned team, but they have a special exemption owing to the length of time they've been structured that way. Legally this is known, charmingly and entirely appropriately, as 'grandfathering'.

Despite this, and unlikely as it seems, a self-selecting group of rich, largely white, largely older men, seem to have managed to look after a sport better than a much more democratic, open system. For all its principled flaws, it's just one of those things – like the BBC – that works and that is better than any known alternative. Not least because it's a form of governance – a collective of owners and a strong players' union constitutionally bound to cooperate – that, unlike the notionally democratic structures of UEFA and FIFA, is able to withstand the corrosive impact of bribery, personal fiefdoms and the entryist power of new money.

It may well be, of course, that the model isn't replicable; that is rests on a culture maintained by a handful of decent people who are on a lucky streak of good commissionerial appointments. One day, perhaps, the barbarians will overrun the NFL as they have football.[51]

All of this is not to say that many old-time Football League club chairmen weren't also creeps and crooks, of course. But at least they were local crooks. The kind of people more likely to bankrupt the local printworks or overcharge tenants for repair work rather than, say, laundering £55m of triad-linked criminal proceeds.

With respectably mediocre clubs like Leicester or Reading or Cardiff being run by the viciously rich, football is like watching the donkeys on Blackpool beach being saddled for the Grand National by supermodels. They're all too old and broken-backed for it all; too clapped out and worn down.

And so am I. I don't want change. I miss Doug Ellis, for heaven's sake. I miss Robert Chase, Peter Swales and Bill Archer.

Local derby, 1965.

At the bottom, the shameless embrace of their new feudal overlords by fans of Manchester City, Chelsea and the like comes from the idea that you will be a happier football fan if your team wins more. This is a seductive but completely false notion.

In the short term, yes, it may prove so. But when winning becomes all your team does for you – when it no longer provides cultural capital, local identification, reinforcement of the self – then it becomes just a brand to be bought into, stuck with and, eventually, inevitably, abandoned. In future, we will change our football clubs like we change mobile phones.

And why, in all of this, would anyone – sane or otherwise – want to own a football club? An NFL team, sure: they're hugely profitable.[52] But a Premier

---

52 And this is real profitability, by the way, when income comfortably exceeds all outgoings, not the Premier League version of financial management where you're doing well if wages are below 100 per cent of turnover and you don't have to dress up a subsidy as sponsorship. None has gone bankrupt recently. And by recently, I mean, well, never.

League club? Few turn a profit – the Glazers aside, who made out like bandits when buying Manchester United.[53]

And certainly some of the most egregious owners – Abramovich, Usmanov, Mansour – are clearly not profiting.

So, why else? Because you love the club and the town and you want to give something back? It does happen: very honourable mentions to Steve Gibson and Dave Whelan.[54] But what if you're not from Middlesbrough or Wigan? Perhaps you want a club like you want a Lamborghini car or a Patek Philippe watch; because that's the thing for rich people to have. The losses it makes aren't a business failure, they are just the cost of running a toy, like the price of fuel for your private plane. It isn't supposed to make money – it just feels nice to own.

The best-case scenario, then, is that our football clubs are owned by effete billionaires too addled by wealth to find any real meaning in their lives. The worst-case scenario is that our national game has become a crucial part of the image-laundering strategy of thieves and thugs.

Last season, Manchester City (owned and sponsored by the Abu Dhabi royal family, who preside over a regime criticised for nepotism, lack of personal and political freedom and widespread human rights abuses) faced Barcelona (owned notionally by their fans, but sponsored by the Qatari royal family... who preside over a regime of nepotism, lack of personal and political freedom and widespread human rights abuses). It was hard to know who to cheer for, but judging from the number of shirts you see worn in London parks on a weekend it's clear that, at least for the moment, Barcelona washes whiter than Manchester City.

The massive turnover in team ownership has also created a toxic legacy for football that goes beyond obscene wages, bankrupt clubs and disenfranchised supporters. It's poisoned our very notion of what acceptable behaviour is, promoting the idea that anything done at work in the pursuit of advancement is acceptable, no matter how tainted that money is.

Take Brian McDermott, the widely respected former Reading manager who was lauded for his dignified response to the insanity at Leeds. About his sacking, Henry Winter tweeted that, while he may not be a first rate manager, he was 'an honourable man' and his sacking had been 'shameful'.49 Winter was re-tweeted hundreds of times and many other journalists and fans expressed similar views.

Don't get me wrong, I love Brian McDermott and I think he seems one of the nicest, most genuine and ablest managers in the game. But 'honourable' is an interesting term to apply to McDermott or any other manager working for a flighty, demanding billionaire of questionable background and limited

---

53 It will be interesting to see how much money Manchester United deliver to their shareholders in future. Will history judge the Glazers to be investing geniuses or, like Carlos Queiroz, John O'Shea and so many others, mere golden egg collectors; innocent bystanders in their own success who just happened to be around the ever brooding Sir Alex Ferguson in his awesomely productive prime?

54 Two mentions of the word 'honourable' in one chapter in connection with Dave Whelan. That's how we used to see him.

patience. Honourable compared to their bosses, perhaps, but what of their own personal morality?

Brian McDermott's CV is worth reviewing. He got his first league managerial job from Sir John Madejski, Reading's benefactor who, when he sold his Auto Trader business, spent 18 months living in Malaysia, which had the side-effect of minimising his huge tax liability on the deal. This great patriot would later sell Reading to the man who fired McDermott: the son of a Russian oligarch. Unjustly dismissed after massively over-achieving, McDermott sought out the tranquillity of a stable club, accepting a role at Leeds, then owned by a Dubai venture capital firm. Later, he would be fired by an Italian fraudster who didn't even own the club.

So this decent man, this bastion of footballing integrity, took a high-paying, high-prestige job with a basketcase club knowing that if it went wrong – if he got fired, if the club went under owing to its dodgy owners – he'd still get paid and, if it went right, he would be able to re-ascend the managerial ladder.

Why then are we supposed to feel sorry for him? If you work as court jester to a king, you shouldn't count on getting a gold watch for long service.

McDermott was just the latest manager to take on a job with bad employers, safe in the knowledge that he, at least, would be fine. You may not think he did wrong, but only in a moral void of a sport would this appear an example of upstanding behaviour. What I'd like to hear about is the managers who turned down the jobs on the basis that clubs shouldn't be run like that or they don't want to pay their mortgage with the blood-stained money of dispossessed and impoverished people around the world. Not sure there are many left like it these days.

There probably weren't in the good old days either, but then the stakes seemed smaller. Work for a hated football chairman then and the worst that might happen is you found yourself being booed in the supermarket while buying milk. Now, shake a chairman's hand and you find yourself co-opted into a public relations campaign designed to win public acclaim for a class of robber barons whose wealth corrupts every country it touches, leaving behind it dictatorship, oppression and poverty.

So let us stop pretending that footballers and managers are one of us. They are prostitutes, as morally culpable for the actions of their gangmasters as anyone who works for a cigarette company is for spreading cancer.

'Those who make peaceful revolution impossible,' said John F. Kennedy, 'will make violent revolution inevitable.' So, while we wait for the blood of the super-rich to run in the streets, let us turn our attention to saving football – for it's not finished yet if we are brave enough to take radical measures.

Our best hope is the mooted European super league. Chelsea, Manchester United, Arsenal, Manchester City, go on, do one! Let us wave them off into the sunset and then, by stirring up the Football League to militancy, bring the rump of the Premier League to its knees. Beg for readmission to the league will be the message, or be cut adrift.

In the future all clubs must be, if not community-owned, then locally-owned by individuals or companies that are themselves wholly owned and tax resident in the UK. There must be a salary cap and a minimum number of homegrown, British players in every team. There must be a partial return to standing and generous concessions for youth season tickets.

And, above all, outside every ground in the country there must be a statue of Ian Culverhouse to remind us that one of the many things more important than winning is the preservation of our clubs as community assets to be reminisced fondly about by future generations.

18.

'I feel numb. Too much is not enough.'

Because every day isn't game day.

THE study of footballing decay is a lifelong obsession for Arsene Wenger. Like a bomb disposal engineer, whose mettle depends on an ability to stick out an uncertain situation for the longest period of time, the true test of nerve for a football manager is the ability to ship out a star player right before he explodes into an expensive mess of paceless sprints, early substitutions and niggling muscle pulls.

Each morning Wenger stands at the gates in London Colney, ostensibly to welcome his players. But as each passes by, his keen nose probes like an explosives-sniffing bee for even the lightest suggestion of taint, terrified another of his cherished stars may be about to turn like raw meat in the sun.

'I'm sorry, Manu, I'm going to have to let you go.'

Wenger's exquisitely sensitive palate – developed during his time in Japan, where he learnt the ancient art of fugu fish preparation – is a cause of unending sadness to him. Like a dog that predicts earthquakes, he has been known to give his condolences to people who didn't yet know themselves to be terminally ill (infamously, Patrick Vieira one day inadvertently applied some of his wife's perfume while dressing for training, and his fate was sealed).

If Wenger detects the smell – that sweet hint of lily, the whiff of spent cordite, the rotting jockstrap of impending physical corruption – he takes Boro Primorac to one side and briefs him to alert agents to a player's availability. He then retreats to his office, weeping bitterly for 24 hours, mourning the loss of another favourite son (and Wenger does love his players – not like Ferguson, who loved them as unruly children who needed the strap – but like Henry Higgins loves Eliza Doolittle: as an experiment to which he's grown too attached. And this despite modern footballers having all the simpleness of Makka Pakka but none of his contented charm).

The Germans have a word for the nature of Wenger's sensory condition, 'effenberg', meaning something that is both a gift and a burden. Sadly, until footballing decay can be better measured, and until the full cost of holding a player too long can be quantified, managers and pundits will continue to pretend that age-related decline is random and focus instead on the far easier task of identifying promising players with the potential to improve.

Past his best?[55]

In recent decades, attention has been paid to the notion of the half-life of information – the period of time in any subject area when 50 per cent of established learning has become obsolete. In many fields of endeavour, the

---

55 In March 2014, the Bayern captain completed 134 of 134 passes as his team clinched the title against Hertha. One hundred per cent passing completion? The only way is down. Or is it?

half-life can be measured in decades. In computing, it's just five years. Even those pursuits of the mind less susceptible to rapid change – like history and philosophy – still measure their half-lives within the length of a career, meaning that if you stick around long enough, you will see much of what you learned and helped develop professionally become redundant (Alex Ferguson has recently been introduced to this idea).

In football, the half-life of a player – the time it takes for him to become half as good as he is currently – is harder to determine. The best current estimate for a top player is three hours and 51 minutes, which is the time it takes to drive from the Emirates to the Etihad.

Historian Arnold J. Toynbee would've understood about half-lives. An academic star of the first half of the 20th century and, in the post-war period, a best-selling public intellectual, his star waned in the 1960s and he found himself forgotten decades before his death. He's now best, if rarely remembered, for attacking the notion that history is 'just one damn thing after another'.

How fortunate that he didn't live long enough to see the development of the Premier League, which lives in a perpetual twilight of ceaseless, meaningless activity.

When I was a youngster, my dad would complain that football was on 'all the bloody time'. This was before the satellite TV and internet revolution, when all you could get on the box was *Saint and Greavsie, Match of the Day*, the FA Cup Final and the occasional live game on a Sunday afternoon. Christ knows how he'd manage now, when football is, in fact, on all the bloody time.

Crowded out by football: kindly government bumblers and wily Morse nurturers.[56]

---

56 On the rare occasion when my wife can't find a show about babies, weddings, celebrities or home improvements on the TV, she'll say, 'Oh, look, the football's on. Would you like to watch it?' Sadly, it's always Newcastle against Debrecen. Always. Never satirical political TV or a middle-brow British murder drama, both of which I like.

The 2012/13 Premier League season ran for 275 days from Saturday 18 August to Sunday 19 May. That's 380 league games in just over 39 weeks. But, of course, that's not the full story of English football. If you add in Champions League, Europa League, FA Cup and League Cup fixtures falling during the league season, there were 546 competitive games featuring at least one Premier League team.

Compare this with the NFL season in 2012/13, which lasted from Wednesday 5 September to Sunday 3 February – 152 days. That's 268 games to be played in just under 22 weeks.

Divide the total number of games by the length of the week in seasons and the figures aren't too far apart – 12.3 games a week in the NFL and 13.9 games a week featuring Premier League clubs.

The significant difference is how and when these games are scheduled. In the NFL they played on just 54 of 152 days – giving about 2.5 match days a week. In English football they played on 156 of the 275 days of the season – about 3.9 match days a week.

But even that's not the end of it, because 46 days were blocked out during the season to create space before and after England's international friendlies and World Cup qualifiers. In fact, then, competitive football featuring at least one Premier League club was played on 156 of 229 days – meaning that there were 4.8 match days a week.

So, despite a broadly similar number of games being played per week, if you switch the TV on in Britain during the football season, you're nearly twice as likely to find a competitive fixture on than if you do so during the NFL season.

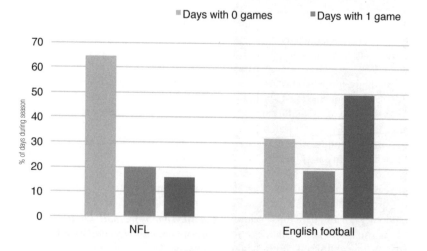

The NFL still broadly maintains the following shape: one game each on Thursday and Monday night, and everything else on a Sunday. In fact, across the 2012/13 season, 92.5 per cent of games were played on a Sunday. In other words, if you follow the NFL one day a week you will be up with the game. You then have a week to process that week's goings on.

In the Premier League, just 57.3 per cent of games were played on Saturday. Devote more of your time to them – say, the whole weekend, and you would have seen just 81.2 per cent of league games. If you had wanted to keep up with all the competitions, the sheer number of games made it all but impossible. Only 43.6 per cent of all fixtures involving a Premier League team (domestic and European cups included) took place on a Saturday, rising to 63.9 per cent if you included the whole weekend. Football is well on the way to filling every single waking hour outside the nine-to-five.

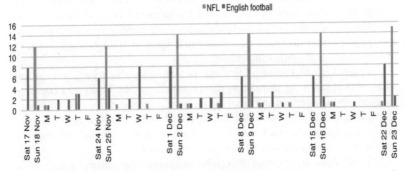

Take a typical month from the 2012/13 season. The sheer number of evenings you have to be available to watch football is just numbing.

Now, the other way of seeing all of this, of course, is that more football is always better and always being able to switch on the TV and see a game is the aim. For a few ultras, perhaps. But it reduces the capacity of the rest of us to engage with the totality of the game, understand it and – above all – manage to maintain a life away from football. By the time the knockout stages of the Europa League arrive in early February, watching football becomes disorientating and overwhelming, like a compilation of The Edge's guitar solos on endless, numbing loop, melting one into another, barely distinguishable. Increasingly, football is becoming the world's first subliminal sport, racing past game after game, too fast to be noticed and appreciated on any conscious level.

Of course, if football is on all the time, cumulatively you do watch more of it. But I'd argue you watch it in a listless, disposable way (I used to do the ironing on a Sunday afternoon to repeats of Lewis. Now I do it midweek when Manchester City are playing).

Your engagement with your team is reduced as your exposure to the sport increases because, while you can always watch football whenever you want, you are unlikely to be able to watch all of your team's games. It casualises your fandom, even as it demands ever more of your attention.

If you doubt me, I challenge you to get a magnifying glass, focus on the chart below and scroll carefully along its full length. It's all the competitive football fixtures played by Premier League teams in one year.

Most of all, football now lacks the narrative arc or coherence of the NFL season. The containment of American football fixtures to Sunday gives time for contextualisation and reflection, not just match reports. It ensures that, unlike in the UK, where the main sports story on almost every day of the week will be the report of a match that ended unexpectedly well (or badly) for a big team, the back papers will be absorbed by analysis, build-up and interpretation.

In the US, they have a great deal more time and space to fill, which means highlights and previews alone won't cut it. One consequence is an increase in bogus stories and manufactured nonsense, but it also creates space for intelligent analysis and attempts to not just explain what happened, but to make sense of it.

The shape of the season too lends itself more naturally to having a grasp of everything rather than racing hectically to keep up with the ever-accelerating efforts of the goal-generating industry.

Listen, I'm old. I make no apology for feeling lost. At my age it is natural to want to break things up to make them comprehensible. That's how I manage with telephone numbers and other big pieces of information, like my children's birthdays. Mercifully, instead of hundreds of fixtures, the NFL has 17 chunks of them, helpfully named Weeks 1 to 17. Each team gets one week off, creating the 16-game season, which is followed by the play-offs.

This format means, even with eight divisions in two conferences, that one always has a ready perspective on where one is during the season. NFL coaches sub-divide their season and judge progress in four quarters of four, with the last being the 'stretch', equivalent to football's 'run-in'.

Symbol of football's cut-throat, phallocentric, families-and-communities-be-damned approach to televising the sport.

The footballing calendar has a series of much more arbitrary sub-divisions, like the terms at a private school. There is the end of October, which marks the end of the beginning of the league and the opening of the sacking season; the Christmas period, by which one's fate is generally deemed to have been cast; February, the month in which Arsenal's title challenge blows up and the league's foreign players are divided into the righteous and the benighted by the wet midweek nights (the Roman month Februarius being named after the Latin term februum, meaning purification); the middle of March, which is the hallowed squeaky bum time; and finally May, during which key players will injure themselves in preparation for any forthcoming international tournament.

And, after all that…nothing.

Modern football runs at full power for four-fifths of the year and then it goes dead. It demands continuous attention and then it gives you a long, dull off-season. Presumably this is to give fans and journalists, as much as players, a chance to recover.

The NFL, meanwhile, shifts gear out of season with a series of deadlines and events to pique the interest without demanding extensive viewing time. Key among these are the draft (which focuses minds on young talent), free agency (which focuses minds on the middling and journeymen talent and the business aspects of salary cap management) and roster cut-down day, where clubs have to produce their final list of 54 players (which focuses minds on bit-part players).

While the supposed news value of these events is played up by TV stations with schedules to fill and by league executives desperate to monetise the game year round, there is a valuable side-effect of having a series of non-game focused events and a long off-season: fan education.

The draft alone produces a situation where NFL fans know more about the physique and technique of amateurs playing in college than most Premier League fans know about their own youth team or the stars of the lower leagues. Likewise, the intricacies of free agency and the salary cap produce a much greater knowledge about the business of running a team and how to manage player contracts.

At the heart of this, I think, is an intrinsic belief in the NFL of the specialness of each game and a determination to defend that by managing and exploiting TV, rather than simply accepting the highest price. The NFL long ago learned that a smart monopoly supplier can dictate more than just the total value of the contract.

LA, America's second largest city, has no NFL team…[57]

It has, for example, a range of stipulations designed to prevent big teams from swamping the coverage of small teams and to defend the interests of all teams.

---

57 Imagine if Birmingham had no worthwhile footballing activity.

My favourite of these is the TV blackout rule. Like football matches, going to an NFL game is an ever-more expensive business, especially compared with the cost and comfort of watching at home. To prevent owners pushing ticket prices up too high or failing to invest in stadium facilities, and to stop fans gradually drifting away from the live experience, any game that isn't sold out 72 hours before it's played won't be shown on TV in the team's home region. This would be like a West Ham–Liverpool game that wasn't sold out by Thursday being available everywhere but London and the south-east on Saturday.

'That goal was grrrrreat!'[58]

The NFL, then, recognises that while an ever-larger percentage of its audience will necessarily be watching on TV, a full house – with the atmosphere that brings – is an essential component of a successful sporting fixture.

And it's working. Ratings for the NFL are sky-high and climbing. In the autumn of 2013, the 24 most watched TV broadcasts in the US were all NFL games, each drawing over 20m viewers.[54]

In the UK this level of success would immediately raise the obvious question: if this many people watch it on a Sunday, why don't we also put it on on Friday and Saturday as well? There are a number of reasons why the NFL doesn't expand beyond Sunday, but two important ones are high school American football, which is traditionally played on Friday nights, and college American football, which is traditionally played on Saturday.

Owing to a number of factors – the US's relative lack of professional sport teams, the way school and college sport act as youth development leagues, the population's lasting attachment to their alma maters – community and amateur sport is a much more important activity in the US than it is over here. Important, in fact, to a level where the NFL would not want to be seen trying to crush it. Imagine if the only football played on a Sunday really was Sunday league football. And that brings me to a curious point about football in the UK.

---

58 Even when it's just flat-out wrong, there's still much to be learnt from the NFL. Like just how ridiculous and shaming name changes are. Just ask fans of the Arizona Cardinals, a team that has also been known, among other names, as the Racine Cardinals, the Chicago Cardinals, the St Louis Cardinals and, until 1993, the Phoenix Cardinals. This most recent change reflected little more than a move across town.

Football is personal and national, but not local – it's core to our national identity (and to some cities' identities), but not to local communities.

Put simply, people don't watch many amateur sports in the UK, especially football. Drive past any park on a Sunday morning and most games – youth or adult – will have more players than spectators. It's a pretty odd thing, that, isn't it? A sporting contest with no wider ramifications, not even of interest to the family of the players. Football is only about football, NFL is about community and people.

For an English audience convinced that the NFL is a made-for-TV pantomime this seems hard to accept, but you can test it by comparing the quality of the cultural output that football and American football inspire. With the enormously honourable exception of anything created by David Peace, football never threatens to spill beyond fictional touchlines into real people's lives.

Kiss this guy...[59]

Compare the greatest TV shows made about football and American football, *Jossy's Giants* and *Friday Night Lights*, and you see one similarity – they're about high-school-age players – and innumerable differences. Most notably, one is a farce about children for children while the other is a drama about small town life for adults. Even the sadly departed Sid Waddell would've admitted which was a richer, more powerful show.

---

59 There were only ten episodes of *Jossy's Giants* made and I watched all of them once and once only when they were first broadcast. In the 27 years between then and researching this piece, I'd always thought the key line of the theme tune was 'We're called Jossy's Giants, football's just a friendship science.' Not strictly meaningful, but potent, I'm sure you'll agree, like the bad poetry of a superior power ballad. Turns out, the line was 'football's just a branch of science', which is both utterly untrue and perfectly captures the emotional and personal hermitry of the game.

The only man in town.[60]

The NFL, then, lends itself to drama, a grand game of scenes and acts. Football, meanwhile, is fit only for structured reality, churning out hours of entirely predictable cultural gruel season after season until the format collapses in on itself, so overripe that even TV executives will soon dare not ask you to spend five nights a week with it in your living room.

---

60 *Friday Night Lights* is a show about fatherlessness. From 'Smash' Williams and Tyra Collette (neither of whom have a dad), to Matt Saracen (whose dad is on the run from his paternal duty in the military), to Buddy Garrity (the cheating, feckless manchild father of Lyla and Buddy Jr), to Vince Howard (whose newly paroled dad threatens his chances of a ticket out of town), to Becky Sproles (whose itinerant dad abandoned the family), to Tim Riggins (with a runaway dad and an incompetent brother in loco parentis) to J.D. McCoy (the hot-housed single child whose domineering father is trying to live out his dreams through his son's talent), fatherlessness in all its literal and metaphorical options is played out leaving one man – Eric Taylor – not only to coach the kids but, with his wife, teacher Tami, to parent an entire town. The role of the manager in British youth football, by contrast, is to promote his son's career at the expense of his other players and try to prevent parents assaulting each other during the game.

19.

'When I was green in judgment: cold in blood...'

On leaving your club – a last word on football.

LIFE experiences have a high opportunity cost. This is important to remember whenever someone says something that, if not actually a disguised form of 'everything happening for a reason', could be read as suggesting that all experiences, even the bad ones, help make us the people we are. According to the internet, Deepak Chopra believes, 'Whatever relationships you have attracted in your life at this moment, are precisely the ones you need in your life at this moment. There is a hidden meaning behind all events, and this hidden meaning is serving your own evolution.'

Clearly he is not a fan of a lower-division football team.

Even wiser than Michael.[61]

---

61 'The greatest mystery of the universe,' Mr Chopra has never said, 'is not how this rose, and the heart-breaking beauty it transmits, could be the product of natural, unguided processes, but why existence should ordain that I abandon a career in medicine, where I actually helped people, to line my pockets selling trite, life-sapping homilies.'

It needs to be recognised that it is possible to make bad mistakes that drain the most precious commodity: time. Yes, crap jobs and bad relationships help make us who we are. That's the problem. How much better would I be if I'd had good jobs? Wetting my pants in school assembly, aged six, undoubtedly contributed to my character. How much better if, instead, I'd been Joseph in the nativity play and had a strong left foot and a good engine?

My former football club is now owned by a Thai billionaire who, on buying the club, was reported to have expressed a desire to return it to the Premier League. A worrying ambition since, given Reading's fanbase, a prolonged stay in the top flight can only realistically be accomplished by spending money the club doesn't have. No fan should welcome this.

Before that, Reading were owned by an oligarch. Or rather by the son of an oligarch ('Oh, Dad, a football club! You shouldn't have!'). The oligarch's father – who, imagine the shame, may not even be a billionaire – owns a huge slice of logging and paper production in Russia. He must have been one hell of a lumberjack.

'When I IPO these trees, I'm going to be a paper millionaire.'

In this chapter, in a slight break with the format of the rest of the book, I've decided to write not about English football, its myriad problems and the role that American football has taken in rekindling my love for sport (if I were a recently separated movie star, I would be said to be 'being comforted by the NFL').

Instead I'm going to write about my break with the football club that I supported for 25 years. This is, rather than a compare and contrast with the NFL, a eulogy for my club and our national sport.

There are few real epiphanies in our lives. Most knowledge is not a dramatic recognition, but a slowly dawning awareness – like Mario Balotelli smelling smoke in his bathroom. It's the sad feeling you get when you realise you've fallen out of love, the gnawing pity you experience thinking of Arsene Wenger and the certain knowledge – which you know he shares – that he'll never again win the Premier League.

These convictions, far from being the conscious product of your subtle and fluid mind, are really just the moment your subconscious finished processing a long stream of impressions, emotions and ideas and kicked the result upstairs for its red carpet premier. You are a government minister; your brain is the wily Sir Humphrey awaiting the perfect opportunity to present to you as your idea a policy document that he has been working on for months.

'I should like to formally register the fact that I have experienced a growing sense of dissatisfaction with the way this club is being run.'

A friend of mine, a former Liverpool fan, knew it was over when listening to the tone-deaf support offered to Suarez after his abuse of Evra. For one of the world's great clubs to take the corporate decision to turn racism into a collective rallying point was too much, even for a man who'd suffered through the Roy Evans years.

For a colleague who was a Charlton fan, it was the ceaseless sniping by fans at Alan Curbishley as, season after season, a promising autumn and early winter gave way to a weak spring. 'He's taken us as far as he can,' they rightly pointed out, their analysis flawed only in that it failed to recognise that he'd taken them as far as he or any other manager, living, historical or fictional could. Gradually my colleague drifted away from his team.

For another friend, a fan of Wrexham – a team with no mean history of underachievement (having never played in the top flight and spent fewer than 15 seasons in the top two tiers of English football) – it was the simple recognition that he was the fan of a club that would never in his lifetime be able to dream of first- or second-tier football without a huge injection of funds of questionable provenance.

For him the issue was simple: if it comes down to a position where the only way small clubs can progress is with a billionaire's generosity; if football no longer allows for minnows to survive and flourish on the funds they can generate at the turnstile; if football is now a game where the table stakes exclude all but whales, then he does not want to play. 'Screw 'em,' he says. 'Let them take their ball home and play by themselves.' Any idiot stupid enough to pay to watch a rich man's ego being stroked is someone with whom he doesn't wish to associate.

Football is dead to him and there's no point having a prolonged grieving process over it. Me, I'm still furious and intent on holding an inquest into the circumstances of its passing. We were together for 25 years. I'm owed an explanation.

A few years ago I was clearing out a cupboard and I found a baggy of grass. Grass from the turf of the old stadium, mind. Browned and brittle, it had a neatly typed note inside – typed by me, though I'd forgotten all about it. It read, 'Centre circle, 30 April 1994'. On that day, when promotion had been secured, we'd had two pitch invasions – one before the end of the game, when we'd scored the goal that sealed it, and one on the final whistle. Such was the determination of the fans to celebrate that the stewards hadn't been able to get everyone back on to the terraces. Instead, like an incoming tide, we lapped the touchline for the final few minutes before pouring on to the pitch, shouting, clapping, hugging and, in my case, getting a souvenir of what still stands as my favourite footballing moment.

It invites disbelief, but I promise you I wrote the first draft of the chapter on 29 April 2014. My best footballing memory, then, was just about to have

Memories: worth their weight in gold.

its 20th birthday. And what a memory it was. If it did nothing else for me but create this one perfect afternoon, I could never hate my former club, only become sadly indifferent to it.

Ultimately it's not foreign owners that weaken the bonds between club and fan, nor is it results, or a manager who preaches ugly football, or an overpriced player, or a new stadium with the name of a supermarket, or the new kit designed by the new owner's eldest son. It's your fellow fans. More specifically, their quiet acquiescence – or open welcome – of money's bloodless coup.

Because despite many fans proclaiming their detestation of our kleptocrat overlords, most of them showed little resistance the moment they caught the whiff of fresh cash about a prospective owner.

Indeed, like the scuttling quislings they are, fans frequently celebrated the arrival, welcoming the sound of Prada jackboots on the path and the Year Zero approach to distasteful virtues like patience, prudence, fairness, solidarity and sharing. All the things we are taught as children but spend our entire adult lives in flight from.

In this new order, success is compulsory and need not be earned, only paid for. Next year is more important than next decade. There is no such thing as too much. The cups are for losers. Devil take the little teams.

Roman and friends share a joke about the current value of the rouble.

As recently as the early 1990s (which feels frighteningly recent to me), small children would bring to the ground – and be admitted with – milk crates to stand on. A game had to be stopped when a gentleman put his still-smouldering pipe in his jacket pocket and caused a fire alert in the seated area. A teenager's season ticket cost £80. My friends and I would be hoarse to the point of speechlessness the day after a game. I went to away games, even reserve games sometimes. There was a local boy in the team; one that I'd actually played against in school games. And, when they closed the Kop for standing, despite us barely ever having played Liverpool, there was a spontaneous chorus of 'You'll never walk alone'. There really was, and I wasn't the only one moved to tears.

In these now-wilted salad days, clubs were still the basic unit of the game, not players and certainly not owners. Players were still the maltreated, lionised, indentured labourers of Gary Imlach's wonderful *My Father and other Working Class Football Heroes*.[53] Managers, meanwhile, as they remain, were ancient pagan kings, elevated to despotic power, later to be dismembered by the masses when the crops failed. Only back then they got till their second or third barren summer before regicide; after one failed harvest it was necessary only to sacrifice the goalless centre-forward.

Dennis Potter said one should look back on one's youth with a tender contempt. He was right. I was an idiot back then, of course, full of foolish certainties. And football, too, was absurd – grown men assembling on a decaying industrial estate to yell filthy abuse at sportsmen, threaten each other with violence and proclaim their town's superiority over places like Runcorn and Rotherham.

But the things I valued then weren't contemptible. The things I loved about football – community, fellowship, camaraderie, unrewarded struggle, joyful celebration – they remain precious and scarce (and the singing; my god, the singing! Four thousand people cleansing themselves of the frustrations of life and raising their voices to a greater cause. Twenty-five thousand at the new place never made that noise. They yell, they shout, they cheer – but they don't *sing*).

I miss it all, not because I've grown up, but because football has. I still value what I loved about football and my team, I just don't find them there any longer. Gradually I drifted away from my club. A season ticket, became a regular visit, become a day trip three or four times a year and then, finally, second-hand fandom through the web.

There comes a time in every aging sports fan's life when he or she must decide if they can still commit to their team. Maybe, once a decade, a hum emerges from the team, a low throb that becomes a roar, and they must ask themselves, 'Despite all the previous disappointments; despite the odds; despite the opposition and the forthcoming fixtures; despite the lack of money and the certain knowledge that the team isn't good enough, isn't even as good as the last team that failed; despite that lack of stars and the still-not-full stadium; despite all I've learned about the game and about myself, is this perhaps it? And can I still say, "Oh, fuck it…I'm all in! All in on this team; my team!"?'

And the sports fan knows that, if the day comes when they can't go all in, then they're through.

Twenty years to the day after my greatest footballing moment, and with ten years of ever growing frustration at the game, I'm there. Despite Deepak's platitudes, much of those recent years were totally wasted – repetitive, frustrating, borderline compulsive revisiting of lost love.

I'll always be an interested and sympathetic observer but the fire has died. I can no longer be brought low by my team and I can no longer be exalted by them.

Goodbye football, you were my first love. From now on, until the next time, I'm all in with the NFL…

SEASON	PLAYED	WON	DRAWN	LOST	FOR	AGAINST	G/D	POINTS
2013/14	46	19	14	13	70	56	14	71
2012/13	38	6	10	22	43	73	-30	28
2011/12	46	27	8	11	69	41	28	89
2010/11	46	20	17	9	77	51	26	77
2009/10	46	17	12	17	68	63	5	63
2008/09	46	21	14	11	72	40	32	77
2007/08	38	10	6	22	41	66	-25	36
2006/07	38	16	7	15	52	47	5	55
2005/06	46	31	13	2	99	32	67	106
2004/05	46	19	13	14	51	44	7	70
2003/04	46	20	10	16	55	57	-2	70
2002/03	46	25	4	17	61	46	15	79
2001/02	46	23	15	8	70	43	27	84
2000/01	46	25	11	10	86	52	34	86
1999/00	46	16	14	16	57	63	-6	62
1998/99	46	16	13	17	54	63	-9	61
1997/98	46	11	9	26	39	78	-39	42
1996/97	46	15	12	19	58	67	-9	57
1995/96	46	13	17	16	54	63	-9	56
1994/95	46	23	10	13	58	44	14	79
1993/94	46	26	11	9	81	44	37	89
1992/93	46	18	15	13	66	51	15	69
1991/92	46	16	13	17	59	62	-3	61
1990/91	46	17	8	21	53	66	-13	59
1989/90	46	15	19	12	57	52	5	64
TOTALS	1126	465	295	366	1550	1364	186	1690

My life in numbers – 25 years of league football.

20.

'It was meant in a Frankie Howerd style way.'

End-of-season review.
And goodbye.

ENGLISH football is like a flock of birds: a chaotic assembly of low grade brains, with limited awareness of the world, whose individual physical abilities and primitive urges allow them, seemingly miraculously, to create dazzling collective displays.

A season is a long time in football. Ask Ashley Cole or Luke Shaw, Fulham or Southampton, David Moyes or Brendan Rodgers. Reputations rise and fall. Clubs have good or bad seasons. Some records are broken. Amazing new discoveries are made.

But how much of this is real change? How much of it is more than mere interesting wrinkles in the fabric of the sport?

What looks to be an ever-evolving, unpredictable activity can, with another perspective, be seen as an essentially static phenomenon. Like planks in Theseus's boat, the birds in the flock change but the impulses that drive the activity, the environment in which they operate and the outcomes (at a collective level) – in other words, the real truth about the flock – these remain largely the same.

At least, that's my feeling about football.

The essays in the book were originally written between the end of July 2013 and the middle of May 2014 – almost exactly a full football season. So, with that in mind, this final chapter is a look back on what I was writing about to see how, if at all, football changed – and to see if my views, like David Moyes's LinkedIn profile, have undergone some recent developments.

A duopoly emerges?

Is the pool of potential Premier League winners really ever shrinking as I, and former prospective Liverpool owner Robert Kraft, claimed? Even as I wrote chapter 11 Liverpool were just about to embark on – and then spectacularly blow – their best shot at a title in over 20 years.

They got bloody close, though. All the talk was of how good coaching and shrewd recruitment alone could overturn the oligopoly at the top of the table. And Liverpool did play remarkably well, with the core of an excellent young team, an innovative young manager, a striker having a season for the ages and several rivals in transition…and yet they still came up short.

As I write this chapter, Suarez is long departed, ostensibly replaced by Ricky Lambert and Mario Balotelli, and Brendan Rodgers's job is apparently under threat. Leaving aside the unexpected highs and lows of the Rodgers era, and looking at the other sensations of last season – Atletico and their astonishing capture of La Liga – the question that needs answering is not 'Can a financially constrained club ever win the title again?' but 'Could anyone seriously imagine that Liverpool or Atletico could regularly match or better last season's achievements without massive additional resources of the kind they *didn't* spend to get them there?' Not as easy a question to read, I appreciate, but probably a more telling one to try and answer.

Nothing has changed my view, then, that the Premier League is increasingly dominated by an ever-smaller number of clubs. Far from this or next season heralding a breakthrough for Liverpool – or any other team – I think it's more likely that we'll see the emergence of a Spanish-style duopoly, with a cluster of Arsenal, Manchester United and Liverpool as a second tier mini-league.

The most important question in sport, any sport, remains, 'How is talent acquired?' Everything else – how is it coached, paid and organised? – are secondary considerations. If there is a problem here, nothing else functions. And, right now, the primary factor in determining talent is not club size, recent success or managerial ability; it's club ownership. In other words, the status quo in the Premier League changes only as the identity or mood of its clubs' owners changes.

In what is my favourite part of this book, I looked at what would've happened if the Premier League had a draft – which players would've ended up where and how that might've affected teams. Imagine if Glenn Hoddle, when at Wolves, had had Wayne Rooney and Robin van Persie gifted to him. Where might Gareth Bale have started out? And who would Eden Hazard have joined?

In the Premier League this was a pipe dream. In the NFL, however, in 2013/14 a skilfully-drafted young Seattle team won the Super Bowl for the first time in their history, making them the 12th winners in the 22 years since the Premier League was founded.

Money continues to turn football on itself

Money remains a catastrophically harmful addiction that football's administrators seem neither willing to properly condemn nor able to tackle. It is an all-consuming drug that's destroying the character and image of the game, despoiling its history and disenfranchising its supporters.

Above all, the idea of the common good or the long-term have ceased to have meaning.

One of the most corrosive effects of this uncontrolled financial excess is the risk-taking it encourages in smaller teams. Recently we saw Championship clubs pleading for a loosening of the Financial Fair Play rules. 'Give us just a little more time,' they begged, like problem gamblers asking for a bigger overdraft but without a promise to quit the casino.

Bad money drives out good. Fulham were acquired by Shad Khan, whose supposed multi-sport masterplan presumably didn't originally include making a string of bad appointments on the way to becoming the first person to simultaneously run clubs in both England and the NFL into the ground.

Meanwhile, in Birmingham, Randy 'slow' Lerner finally realised the folly of trying to compete financially with the big beasts and put Villa up for sale. Early indications are that his eight years in charge may leave him with little return on his investment.

Further down the pyramid there are tales of financial woe at Leicester, Blackburn and Wolves, and even suggestions that QPR may have borrowed against future season's ticket sales. Reading – once, I fondly imagined, many people's second favourite club – found themselves deeply in debt, having borrowed against TV future payments in a doomed effort to stay in the Premier League, apparently believing that their oligarch owner would be able to cover any shortfall. But, like a person who orders steak and then professes poverty when the bill arrives, money suddenly became an issue and the club had to go and look for a new sugar daddy. Plus ça change.

These kind of cheap friends with expensive tastes are usually quite fun to go out with occasionally, and you can tolerate one or two in your social group, but football has seen far too many people recently with short arms and deep pockets, snapping their fingers at waiters and calling for champagne, barely able to afford a taxi home at the end of the night.

From small clubs to feeder clubs

Almost as soon as I'd finished writing about the endangered dignity of lower-division football and how the insatiable thirst of the Premier League – manifested through the Elite Player Performance Plan – threatened its very existence, up popped Ed Woodward. This seemingly innocent and unworldly executive, who will be lucky to make it out of Old Trafford in a sea-plane, mooted the feeder club idea among other monstrously self-interested proposals for 'reforming' football.

A few months later the FA released a report suggesting B teams. Neglecting their responsibilities to grassroots and league football, they seemingly took the view that nothing but nothing must stand in the way of improving the England football team. It's unclear, however, how playing lower-division football for a big club's reserve team is better than playing Premier League football or Championship football for a smaller club.

The FA, it seems, like the Premier League, is committed to doing anything to help young players get more competitive games. Anything, that is, except actually stopping the Premier League hoarding and then neglecting those same young players. By failing to call for stricter rules on foreign players and a domestic salary cap, the best minds in the game are effectively suggesting that all that's preventing the new generation of British players dominating the Premier League and international football is access to coaching. They can't really believe that, can they?

Kudos to Against League 3, among other grassroots campaigners, for challenging the FA on exactly what it's trying to achieve and how it aims to balance the needs of the amateur game, the league set-up and the national side against the domination of the Premier League.

As anyone who's read *Soccernomics* will know, it's questionable whether England does in fact underperform internationally.[54] So why, really, all the emphasis on expanding the numbers of players that Premier League clubs can have? Is sacrificing the integrity of the league a necessary but regrettable measure to secure England's future?[62]

We've long been used to a supine FA, unable to please its numerous stakeholders, but now it seems we have a captured regulator, eagerly currying favour with those it should be attempting to control.

The theatrical farce of Financial Fair Play

Looking at the NFL, it's amply clear that effective financial discipline can't be related to club income. To do so simply entrenches the status quo or invites profligate owners to appoint their ego chief scout in an effort to humiliate the competition.

After years of tough talk, UEFA's first batch of Financial Fair Play fines revealed the true impotence of football's authorities. Manchester City and PSG were found to have failed to fudge their figures sufficiently even to meet UEFA's lax Financial Fair Play targets. The punishment, a €60m fine over three seasons, is less annually than the €36m prize money Manchester United got for going out in the last 16 of the 2012/13 Champions League. In other words, taking its lead from Wall Street deferred prosecution agreements, UEFA has shown that Financial Fair Play fines are not a real deterrent, just a cost of doing business in the modern game.

UEFA made the punishment complex enough that many will have assumed it was a carefully targeted set of smart sanctions. But, no, in the absence of a proper salary cap, fining teams for breaking Financial Fair Play is just the denialist posturing of the defeated bureaucrat.

Most notably, while UEFA's system is based on retrospective assessment of financial reports – something that provides lucrative opportunities for lawyers to delay matters – in the NFL, no contract is valid until the league says it won't breach the cap.

Meanwhile, in the same season that Wayne Rooney got a salary rise to £15.6m a year, the NFL salary cap is to be pushed up to $130m: about £30k a week per player. Or about a third of a James Milner, the prototypical average Premier League player.

---

62 I refuse to believe that club and international football are locked in a zero-sum game. But, if they are, the FA should be careful before it assumes that all football fans would willingly put country before club.

Putting that into context, in 2013, the entire annual pay bill for the BMC Racing squad, supposedly the best-paid team in cycling, was £12.3m. And this, don't forget, is Wayne Rooney who has only outscored midfielder Frank Lampard in four of the last ten seasons. This is Wayne Rooney whose salary in USD is $26m. In 2012/13, Peyton Manning, the NFL MVP (equivalent to PFA Player of the Year), earned $15m. Malcolm Smith, the Super Bowl MVP, earned $0.47m. And Russell Wilson, the Super Bowl-winning quarterback, earned $0.53m.

Football's money madness continues and, I believe, nothing short of a low and hard salary cap will prevent it getting worse. Until that happens, competition will never become fairer, player wages will never come down and ticket prices will never come back within the reach of a person on an average income.

The ever-shortening shelf-life of managers

Something strange is also happening to managers. When I looked at managerial longevity at the beginning of the season, I concluded that it was little worse than in the NFL, the difference being that you are rarely sacked mid-season in the US.

I noticed that the pre-season average for Premier League managers had dipped (from about three seasons to 1.6) because Ferguson's retirement triggered a merry-go-round that left David Moyes and Roberto Martinez, among others, with their feet under new tables. I put this down to a one-off sequence of events, assuming tenure would climb back to the historical average.

By mid-season, though, it was starting to look like I may have been wrong and that using the mean instead of the median had allowed the tenure of a few old-timers, like Arsene Wenger, to distort the true picture.

Consider this stat from January 2014:

> @sportingintel
> Pochettino appointed #SaintsFC manager a yr ago today. He is 42nd longest-serving manager of the 92 clubs: 50 in their jobs less than a year[55]

So it's not just sheikhs from oppressive regimes with itchy trigger fingers. Football managers are increasingly expected to demonstrate success almost immediately – without the opportunity to significantly alter their squad's composition or improve its performance with coaching. Being the chairman of a football club is power without responsibility taken to the extreme.

When a manager is sacked after less than a season, the failure is the board's. And, right now, that means that most English boardrooms are not up to the job. Not least because the clear evidence is that changing managers doesn't work. No matter how it is dressed up, sacking a manager isn't a forward-looking, rational solution to a problem; it is the worst kind of reactive, thoughtless, responsibility-shirking, back-covering.

And, like financial excess, premature sackings are a contagious phenomenon – a product of group-think that is incredibly hard to resist. For this reason, now more than ever, football needs the decision taking out of its hands with a managerial transfer window.[63] By making it harder to fire a manager, you instantly focus minds on the hiring process. Not only would we not have seen David Moyes fired before season's end, but anyone anointing Ryan Giggs as heir apparent after *one* win – an idea mooted in many national papers – would be laughed out of town.

Management, it must be clear by now, is a difficult profession requiring skills rarely found in a former footballer. It's time the game took a close look at how to create a better career path for the managers of tomorrow.

The rise of football analytics

As I noted in my review of *Match of the Day*, laziness is the defining characteristic of the output of the majority of TV pundits. Compared with the great American broadcasters or with a few notable exceptions over here – the imperious Gary Neville, for example – it's clear that simply moving Hansen on didn't change much. Nor did the occasional embarrassing flirtation with Russell Brand and Leonardo.

When I wrote chapter five, I was scathing about football fans' and football writers' commitment to evidence. Having spent the season immersing myself further in it, I see I was only half right. The brilliant practitioners I craved are there, I just hadn't looked hard enough. Ted Knutson of Statsbomb, *The Telegraph*'s Jonathan Liew, the great SportingIntelligence.com, the economics writer Daniel Altman.

They and many more are doing amazing work, creating some remarkable metrics and, taking their lead from baseball and the NFL, interrogating the game in a way that seemed unimaginable ten years ago. Increasingly, their influence is permeating the game and shaping the way we think and talk about it. Long may it continue.

The still-unaddressed question of ownership

The death of William Clay Ford Sr, who'd spent 51 years in charge of Detroit's NFL team, prompted me to write chapter 17 about the importance of stability of ownership. Only weeks after that, Ralph Wilson, another Methuselah of the NFL, died. Wilson's club, Buffalo, was one of the ten NFL clubs that had never changed hands. Together, Ford and Wilson had 105 years of accumulated team ownership. By comparison, at the time of Wilson's death, the total ownership period of *all* clubs in the Premier League was just 152 years.

The ultimate example of ownership insanity is, of course, Leeds United. The club, like an illustrated DSM of footballing madness, displays every known malady affecting the game. Overspending leading to relegation-triggered bankruptcy, repeated managerial and ownership changes, Ken Bates, police investigations, owners without footballing knowledge, opaque finance, on-

---

63 How would this work? Well, perhaps you'd be able to fire your manager at any point, but you'd not be allowed to replace him with someone else currently managing a football team (only out-of-work managers or internal caretaker candidates would be allowed to be appointed). Or, as with restrictions on the number of clubs a player could appear for in a year, no manager would be allowed to manage two clubs in one season.

field failure. With football's finances and administration as they are, you have to question the sanity (and motives) of anyone who wants to own any football club. And yet still people wanted to buy Leeds. Leeds of the executive goldfish; Leeds of the Seth Johnson negotiating gambit; Leeds of the McDermott hokey cokey. Even if, as is claimed, some of these Leeds legends are apocryphal, it's telling that so many attach to one club.

Indeed, only days after I wrote about how ridiculous the current Owner's and Director's Test was, Massimo Cellino – a man with a fraud conviction in his native Italy – won his appeal and took over Leeds. And then later lost. It didn't seem to occur to the administrators of the game that what was embarrassing about these events was not the repeated appeals, reinstatements and suchlike, but the morally impoverished idea that someone's fitness to run a club should depend on a lawyerly interpretation of the legal and tax codes of another country, rather than, say, a thorough assessment of that person's character, plans and means.

Try as it might, though, I'm hopeful that football won't be able to continue to ignore the issue by pushing the idea that everything needs to be handled on a case by case basis. Not least because two of England's largest clubs are owned by people on friendly terms with Vladimir Putin, people who could be snared if the net of sanctions against the Russian regime is cast wider.

Racism, tolerance and conduct unbecoming

Musing on the footballing nostalgia triggered by Barry Glendenning's #IanCulverhouse game, I boldly asserted, 'Outside every ground in the country, there must be a statue of Ian Culverhouse.' Less than a month later, Culverhouse – the man I'd held up as a totem of all that was good in lower-league football – and fellow Villa colleague Gary Karsa, were suspended and then dismissed, allegedly for their aggressive, bullying behaviour. My plan for the statues may take a little longer than expected.

Football continued to skirt clumsily around racism, like a former soap star doing the paso doble on *Strictly Come Dancing*. Even as the number of black and ethnic minority managers fell to zero, there were further depressing indications that football still has one foot in the Dark Ages. As the season progressed we discussed – actually seriously discussed – if 'yid' was *really* a racist term. Elsewhere, abroad, we saw repeated instances of racist behaviour by fans being punished with nugatory fines.

A sport is only as good as the courage and integrity of its administrators. It's a shame then that FIFA, UEFA, the FA and the Premier League are so inept and weak. The point was underlined when LA Clippers owner Donald Sterling was recorded making a series of racist remarks. This elderly, white, billionaire received a lifetime ban from basketball, a $2.5m fine and his team was sold out from under him. Incidentally, the $2.5m fine (the highest allowable under NBA rules) means that, compared with the banana-throwing fine given to Villarreal, certain elements in football regard racism by fans during a game as 150 times less serious than racism by an NBA owner in private.

Meanwhile, while Britain was lauding a transvestite winning Eurovision as an unprecedented moment of tolerance in the history of pop music, in the

US, Michael Sam became the first openly gay player to be picked in the NFL draft. He went in the seventh and final round to St Louis, who in 1946, were also the first team to sign a black player. Talented though Sam is, he didn't make the final squad, signing eventually to Dallas's practice squad. He may play for them, he may get released.

Either way, though, he's made a breakthrough. And, sooner or later, someone even more talented will follow and become the game's first gay star. It may even be that, if Sam becomes a regular for Dallas, other more established NFL players may follow his lead and come out.

Gender equality, however, had a bad year in the US and the UK. Domestic violence, a dark secret of the NFL, was catapulted on to the front pages of every US newspaper by a video of a player punching his girlfriend in a hotel lift. Having been given only a two-game ban before the video came out, the player was suspended indefinitely along with several other big names implicated in violent behaviour towards their wives or children.

Back home in the Premier League, Richard Scudamore exemplified the worst in Britain's clubby, pampered, insular elite, sending a series of sexist e-mails bemoaning the difficulty of dealing with 'irrational women' and getting them 'off his shaft'. Doubtless he will have shortened his career at the Premier League, but again, not because football's authorities really disapprove of that kind of thing. They just don't like being embarrassed.

It is just possible that NFL's and the Premier League's weak initial responses – and the backlashes they created – will end up having taught the powers that be a lasting lesson. Or at least we may hope so.

Still, though – and several years on – we have no firm commitment from the Football League or Premier League to introduce a Rooney Rule or other similar measure targeted directly at the managerial hiring process.

The last days of FIFA

This is the true genius of Sepp Blatter: he has corrupted and compromised football so totally that there's no one left to challenge him.

Look at English football, still huffily denouncing the 2018 World Cup bidding process without acknowledging that it too appears tainted by its participation. Who could we send to FIFA to clean house? 'Lucky' Gordon Taylor, Richard 'Shaft' Scudamore or Greg 'B Team' Dyke?

Fortunately it seems that FIFA may finally have pushed things too far. Change won't come from within the organisation – nor from the wider world of football – but, in taking the world's game and selling it to the highest bidders, people who history will revile as monsters, football's administrators have made it impossible for governments and law enforcement bodies to turn a blind eye any longer. It becomes increasingly clear that the only appropriate response to FIFA's plans for Russia 2018 and Qatar 2022 is their abolition. Together, they will stand as football's Berlin Olympics.[64]

---

64   The IOC, it should be noted, awarded Berlin the 1936 Games *before* the rise to power of the Nazis. Their sin, then, was in failing to move the Games. FIFA, by contrast, knew amply well the character of the governments to which it awarded the World Cup.

No longer can TV audiences pretend that corruption is just low level, largely harmless skimming. FIFA and football are profiting from slavery, theft and abuse of power and those who sponsor, watch or participate in the tournaments must accept their share of responsibility for those host regimes' crimes. The choice really is that stark.

So I'd like to draw your attention to the FIFA constitution. To one particular clause, in fact; my favourite: Clause 86. In one paragraph, it sketches out the way to a new and hopeful future for a better football.

86 Dissolution

If FIFA is disbanded, its assets shall be transferred to the supreme court of the country in which its headquarters are situated. It shall hold these assets in trust as 'bonus pater familiae' until FIFA is re-established.[56]

For a number of reasons – the FBI probe, the planned re-election of Blatter, the winter dates and human rights scandals of the Qatar win, the impending 2018 World Cup in what's becoming an outlaw state – there has never been a better time to attempt the overthrow of FIFA. Let us rally to Clause 86 and hope that, when FIFA finally topples, the shockwaves will be felt at all levels of the game.

Could it be, then, that there is hope still for the Beautiful Game? Could it be that equity, decency, fair competition and responsible ownership aren't relics of the 20th century? Those who care about the sport to the exclusion of all others had better hope so, because the NFL is coming.

It's sending us more games each year, with the promise of a team of our own if we can fill Wembley regularly. Even if you think you could never abandon your football club, as a sports fan, you need at least once in your life to experience a game every bit as visceral and pure as American football. Strip away the pads and the huge teams and the delays and the sheer size of the production and, underneath, you'll find a game based on the most primal of sporting activities – running, throwing, catching, tackling and, yes, kicking.

It's a game where the weakest teams get first dibs on players; where TV money is shared equally; where players get well paid but not excessively so; where it's impossible to predict who will be the best and the worst teams five years from now; and where, above all, every fan can dream of a better future for his or her club.

It's a game that, if you've ever bemoaned the state of football, you might just find has something for you.

So if you're up late one night, put the NFL on for half an hour. Or, better still, come along to Wembley one matchday. Come and discover that you can love sport again. Remind yourself that, rather than a shabby magnet for the avaricious, it can and should be one of the most glorious and uplifting of human undertakings.

I'll see you there.

And, with that, I declare The Ugly Game over.

Endnotes

1   The Guardian, 18 April 2013, http://www.guardian.co.uk/news/datablog/2013/apr/18/premier-league-club-accounts-debt

2   Michael MacCambridge, America's Game: The Epic Story of How Pro Football Captured a Nation

3   Michael MacCambridge, America's Game: The Epic Story of How Pro Football Captured a Nation

4   Squawka-licensed Official Premier League data from Opta, 20 June, 2013, http://www.squawka.com/news/top-10-mostamazing-football-stats-from-the-2012-13-season/11249

5   BBC News Online, 17 April 2013, http://www.bbc.co.uk/sport/0/football/22194042

6   Telegraph, 5 Sep 2011, http://www.telegraph.co.uk/sport/football/competitions/premier-league/8743393/Footballs-dysfunctional-family-must-smash-black-managers-glass-ceiling.html

7   New Yorker, 21 April 2008, http://www.newyorker.com/magazine/2008/04/21/up-and-then-down

8   Adrian Bell, Chris Brooks & Tom Markham (2013) The performance of football club managers: skill or luck?, Economics & Finance Research: An Open Access Journal, 1:1, 19-30, www.tandfonline.com/doi/pdf/10.1080/21649480.2013.768829

9   Quotes reproduced by permission of Guardian News & Media Ltd, The Guardian, 19 October 2011, www.theguardian.com/football/2011/oct/19/football-league-academies

10 BBC, 20 October 2011, http://www.bbc.co.uk/blogs/legacy/paulfletcher/2011/10/football_league_votes_in_favou.html

11 Michael Marmot, Status Syndrome: How Your Social Standing Directly Affects Your Health, Bloomsbury, 2004

12 Sports Business Journal, 19-25 November 2012, http://www.sportsbusinessdaily.com/Journal/Issues/2012/11/19/Leagues-and-Governing-Bodies/NFL-ejections.aspx

13 Premier League, 15 November 2012, http://www.premierleague.com/en-gb/news/news/2012-13/nov/arrests-down-at-premier-league-stadiums/

14 Alcohol – Health Committee, 23 April 2009, http://www.publications.parliament.uk/pa/cm200910/cmselect/cmhealth/151/09042307.htm

15 CTV News, 26 March 2013 http://www.ctvnews.ca/business/why-most-lottery-winners-end-up-losing-their-new-fortune-1.1211569

16 Inside the huddle, 2 July 2012, NFL UK, http://www.nfluk.com/opinions/articles/inside-huddle-podcast-27

17 Herald Scotland, 1 November 2011, http://www.heraldscotland.com/news/home-news/bbc-attacked-over-alan-hansen-s-15m-salary.15650046

18 http://1000000-euro.de/how-much-does-a-million-pounds-weigh/index.php

19 BBC, 22 November 2012, http://www.bbc.co.uk/news/business-20442666

20 Quotes reproduced by permission of BBC Sport, Match of the Day, 19th October 2013

21 BBC, 19 January 2007, http://news.bbc.co.uk/1/hi/england/6278897.stm

22 Premier League, 21 May 2013, http://www.premierleague.com/en-gb/news/news/2012-13/may/premier-league-total-broadcasting-payments-season-2012-13.html

23 The Guardian, 18 April 2013, http://www.theguardian.com/news/datablog/2013/apr/18/premier-league-club-accounts-debt#data

24 The Guardian, 11 April 2013, http://www.theguardian.com/football/2013/apr/11/la-liga-television-rights-premier-league

25 Sporting Intelligence, 21 May 2011, http://www.sportingintelligence.com/2011/05/31/charge-sheet-fifa per centE2 per cent80 per cent99s-murky-dealings-in-the-sepp-blatter-era-310501/

26 On Bullshit, Harry Frankfurt, Princeton University Press, 2005

27 The Chronicle, 12 December 2013, http://www.chroniclelive.co.uk/sport/football/football-news/plan-exclusive-paid-for-newcastle-united-6401153

28 Tim Krul, 7 December 2013, https://twitter.com/TimKrul/status/409355459871907840

29 Tim Krul, 6 October 2013, https://twitter.com/TimKrul/status/386809278335832064

30 Stephen Taylor, 10 November 2013, http://www.steventaylor27.com/spurs-match-10-11-13

31 Stephen Taylor, 12 December 2013, http://www.steventaylor27.com/southampton-14-12-13/

32 BBC, 27 October 2005, http://www.bbc.co.uk/berkshire/content/articles/2005/ 10/27/dave_kitson_feature.shtml

33 Nate Jackson, 21 July 2011, http://deadspin.com/5823549/dear-chris-kluwe-when-we-want-the-punters-opinion-well-ask-for-it-we-wont

34 Chris Kluwe, 22 July 2011, http://deadspin.com/5823788/chris-kluwe-responds-can-i-kick-it-yes-i-can

35 BBC, 2 September 2013, http://www.bbc.co.uk/news/health-23896855

36 Kirk Goldsberry, 30 June 2014, http://grantland.com/the-triangle/crime-and-punishment-should-the-penalty-kick-spot-be-moved-back/

37 https://twitter.com/bglendenning/status/437647497516048384

38 https://twitter.com/bglendenning/status/437673697005277185

39 https://twitter.com/bglendenning/status/437700979560300545

40 https://twitter.com/bglendenning/status/437659084515713024

41 https://twitter.com/bglendenning/status/437687139820904448

42 https://twitter.com/bglendenning/status/437685459163283456

43 https://twitter.com/hoggy_vegas/status/437674131492839425

44 Mark Binelli, The Last Days of Detroit: Motor Cars, Motown and the Collapse of an Industrial Giant, 2014, Vintage

45 Forbes, 14 August 2013, http://www.forbes.com/sites/ mikeozanian/2013/08/14/the-most-valuable-nfl-teams/

46 Forbes, 17 April 2013, http://www.forbes.com/sites/ mikeozanian/2013/04/17/soccers-most-valuable-teams-real-madrid-dethrones-manchester-united-from-top-spot-at-3-3-billion/

47 Independent, 1 July 2013, http://www.independent.co.uk/sport/football/ news-and-comment/roman-abramovichs-10year-chelsea-anniversary-what-did-he-ever-do-for-us-spend-2-billion-in-10-years-at-chelsea-thats-what-8680084.html

48 http://www.thefa.com/~/media/files/thefaportal/governance-docs/rules-of-the-association/2013-14/owners-and-directors-test.ashx

49 Matthew Stewart, The Management Myth: Debunking Modern Business Philosophy, W. W. Norton & Co, 2010

50 Constitution and bylaws of the National Football League, 2006, http:// static.nfl.com/static/content/public/static/html/careers/pdf/co_.pdf

51 https://twitter.com/henrywinter/status/429346769147678720

52 TV by the Numbers, 27 November 2013, http://tvbythenumbers.zap2it. com/2013/11/27/15-nfl-games-top-25-million-viewers-in-2013-nfl-games-two-most-watched-shows-of-the-week/218766/

53 Gary Imlach, My Father and other Working Class Football Heroes, Yellow Jersey Press, 2006

54 Simon Kuper and Stefan Szymanski, Soccernomics, HarperSports, 2012

55 https://twitter.com/sportingintel/status/424500131577090048

56 http://www.fifa.com/mm/document/affederation/bodies/02/06/57/65/ anhangcen.pdf

Picture Credits and Permissions

oy9cNZ-cieUow-ovbebS-6QRD6L-ecbqUh-dG2nF3-6QMz4H-6QMzqZ-
owjQ4P-7acMM4-oucg3f-6QMzkK-6QMzhZ-cieWwW)

p.18 Ronnie Macdonald – licenced under the Creative Commons Attribution
2.0 Generic Licence (www.flickr.com/photos/ronmacphotos/497993910/in/
photolist-L1mju-4cfeYh-L1meU-6RSVm)

p.20 Ben Sutherland – licenced under the Creative Commons Attribution 2.0
Generic Licence (www.flickr.com/photos/bensutherland/8066833420/in/
photolist-dhQCwQ-HkuLM-n4DSi9-HkpPZ-8qTzQM-gMkKCY-ekM5B8-
faQjJY-fx8BYd)

p.20 William Garner – licenced under the Creative Commons Attribution
2.0 Generic Licence (www.flickr.com/photos/68328491@N07/6307366141)

p.21 CmdrGravy – licenced under the Creative Commons Attribution
2.0 Generic Licence (www.flickr.com/photos/cmdrgravy/316561607/in/
photolist-4A25F2-4UCmCg-NPLoS-NPLoW-dNrQne-dNrR96-tYsJK-
a5geSe-a5gghz-a5gegv-a5gfoT-a5j7Ty-a5j6nh-a5gdgT-a5j7mo-a5gfFx-
a5j6Gu-a5j8Hw-a5gcXV-NSRYT-ca6jtS-2ZvuQj-2Zv7mA)

p.22 Angie Six – licenced under the Creative Commons Attribution-
NoDerivs 2.0 Generic Licence (www.flickr.com/photos/
angiesix/7831921340)

p.25 Mark Leech/Getty Images

p.27 Nick Hubbard – licenced under the Creative Commons Attribution 2.0
Generic Licence (www.flickr.com/photos/nickhubbard/15209500126)

p.28 randychiu – licenced under the Creative Commons Attribution 2.0
Generic Licence (www.flickr.com/photos/randychiu/4033667683)

p.29 Napoleon Sarony

p.30 Kojach – licenced under the Creative Commons Attribution 2.0 Generic
Licence (www.flickr.com/photos/kojach/3852120743)

p.31 themostinept – licenced under the Creative Commons Attribution-
Share Alike 2.0 Generic Licence (www.flickr.com/photos/46123010@
N04/7422164890)

p.32 Flavio~ – licenced under the Creative Commons Attribution 2.0
Generic Licence (www.flickr.com/photos/37873897@N06/8042418686)

p.33 DonkeyHotey – licenced under the Creative Commons Attribution 2.0
Generic Licence (www.flickr.com/photos/donkeyhotey/12369090945)

p.34 Adam Jones – licenced under the Creative Commons Attribution-Share Alike 2.0 Generic Licence (www.flickr.com/photos/adam_jones/3793617651)

p.37 smerikal – licenced under the Creative Commons Attribution-Share Alike 2.0 Generic Licence (www.flickr.com/photos/smerikal/5930669742)

p.38 Linda Tanner – licenced under the Creative Commons Attribution 2.0 Generic Licence (www.flickr.com/photos/goingslo/8182913559)

p.39 ChrisTheDude – licenced under the Creative Commons Attribution-ShareAlike 3.0 Unported Licence (en.wikipedia.org/wiki/Corner_kick#mediaviewer/File:BarwellFC.jpg)

p.41 Kurt Bauschardt – licenced under the Creative Commons Attribution-Share Alike 2.0 Generic Licence (www.flickr.com/photos/kurt-b/12597412465)

p.42 Aécio Neves – licenced under the Creative Commons Attribution 2.0 Generic Licence (www.flickr.com/photos/aecioneves/8368413702)

p.45 Matt Lemmon – licenced under the Creative Commons Attribution-Share Alike 2.0 Generic Licence (www.flickr.com/photos/mplemmon/252138009)

p.46 A Healthier Michigan – licenced under the Creative Commons Attribution-Share Alike 2.0 Generic Licence (www.flickr.com/photos/healthiermi/8805838996)

p.49 Gina – licenced under the Creative Commons Attribution 2.0 Generic Licence (www.flickr.com/photos/gdallariva/8561835827)

p.52 Jimmy Baikovicius – licenced under the Creative Commons Attribution-Share Alike 2.0 Generic Licence (www.flickr.com/photos/jikatu/6336552408)

p.52 Erin A. Kirk-Cuomo – licenced under the Creative Commons Attribution 2.0 Generic Licence (www.flickr.com/photos/secdef/8391795159)

p.53 Duncan Hull – licenced under the Creative Commons Attribution 2.0 Generic Licence (www.flickr.com/photos/blogcatatanbola/4973340286)

p.55 Kitmondo Complete Plants – licenced under the Creative Commons Attribution 2.0 Generic Licence (www.kitmondo.com/complete-plants)

p.57 Cory Doctorow – licenced under the Creative Commons Attribution-Share Alike 2.0 Generic Licence (www.flickr. com/photos/ doctorow/2496308570/in/photolist-4NAeyW-3dBGx-bffWWx-31kNDJ-6kiQ1C-ai8vU6-2Zzxj4-6FQwUF-dwQpy-88gYP-dyxMSS-2zfHV-8nNnhs-9gQfuV-9oTyyy-4rnS4f-itprt-7cefCd-8iVDKD-9YB93k-6tbvxn-7j7bYS-45M9B-pm1dHS-pkZc2g-pCe4Ui-pAszvd-pCvgBZ-pCveaV-pCtgMQ-pCt8VY-pCe4d8-pm1b6Y-pkZgw8-5g1eyJ-64zmQ7-6Memyn-7MYUGL-7CcE9-yQ88-cgA1PG-3xzy-xNmdZ-57CiQ2-7mQ6XG-MMwKt-7n747p-c2HYPG-9EQPGt-63dhSi)

p.61 Gareth Saunders – licenced under the Creative Commons Attribution-Share Alike 2.0 Generic Licence (www.flickr.com/photos/ garethjmsaunders/3435161303)

p.63 Marion Doss – licenced under the Creative Commons Attribution-Share Alike 2.0 Generic Licence (www.flickr.com/photos/ooocha/3051171105)

p.65 Department for Business, Innovation and Skills – licenced under the Creative Commons Attribution-NoDerivs 2.0 Generic Licence (www.flickr. com/photos/bisgovuk/6352817321)

p.66 Oli R – licenced under the Creative Commons Attribution 2.0 Generic Licence (www.flickr.com/photos/oli/17859913)

p.67 DIUS Corporate – licenced under the Creative Commons Attribution-NoDerivs 2.0 Generic Licence (www.flickr.com/photos/ diusgovuk/2922178604)

p.68 William Hoare/National Portrait Gallery

p.69 Chad J. McNeeley – licenced under the Creative Commons Attribution 2.0 Generic Licence (www.flickr.com/photos/thejointstaff/4479500323)

p.70 Andrew Carrick Gow: Cromwell Dissolving the Long Parliament, Mackelvie Trust Collection, Auckland Art Gallery Toi o Tāmaki Frame sponsored by John Gow family

p.72 Arcadiuš – licenced under the Creative Commons Attribution 2.0 Generic Licence (www.flickr.com/photos/arcadius/5375874443)

p.73 Pieter van der Heyden after Pieter Bruegel the Elder: Big Fish Eat Little Fish (17.3.859) In *Heilbrunn Timeline of Art History* . New York: The Metropolitan Museum of Art, 2000 http://www.metmuseum.org/toah/ works-of-art/17.3.859

p.74 Henry Walter/National Portrait Gallery

p.136 Hotel Arthur Helsinki – licenced under the Creative
Commons Attribution 2.0 Generic Licence (www.flickr.com/photos/
hotelarthur/8272158148/in/photolist-64KRvG-dAYYqm-aBj2j8-HM916-
5NYZPq-4WNmxD-4WSCDu-4dtfsb-cgUvhC-avUAD-kLUEMz-owdEa6-
HM4uE-7rb63s-dn3iTb-zCptp-nAbjMG-gCPg3-9uggM-jomtED-4-
ZQbWZ-81RwRq-oJekcG-3xyskr-oNFDPu-ny8ogL-3xEgns-5gfmiC-
4X9s7P-oweobD-GcAsG-GcERX-5o3pQL-dL3Pgp-abMLiB-9NKxF6-
4Z9EWn-4fjV8T-bow1Xz-8n7WDv-GcAt9-bovVfi-ofpKm7-ofif6H-
4yEFXB-nY6AnG-2rpFoS-n8Q4uc-d5B2J3-5rHzU4)

p.136 Emi Moriya – licenced under the Creative Commons
Attribution-Share Alike 2.0 Generic Licence (www.flickr.com/photos/
emiemihuimei/4677317599)

p.136 Lordcolus – licenced under the Creative Commons Attribution 2.0
Generic Licence (www.flickr.com/photos/lordcolus/9775464/in/photolist-)

p.140 Dennis Jarvis – licenced under the Creative Commons
Attribution-Share Alike 2.0 Generic Licence (www.flickr.com/photos/
archer10/5269531575)

p.144 Kyle Hailey/wetribe – licenced under the Creative Commons
Attribution 2.0 Generic Licence (www.flickr.com/photos/
kylehailey/462492056)

p.145 Fons Heijnsbroek – licenced under the Creative Commons
Attribution 2.0 Generic Licence (www.flickr.com/photos/city-
amsterdam/10572972474/)

p.146 Charanjit Chana – licenced under the Creative Commons Attribution
2.0 Generic Licence (www.flickr.com/photos/cchana/13999550963)

p.147 Richard Riley – licenced under the Creative Commons Attribution 2.0
Generic Licence (www.flickr.com/photos/rileyroxx/244501355)

p.148 Dragan Tatic – licenced under the Creative Commons Attribution 2.0
Generic Licence (www.flickr.com/photos/minoritenplatz8/8469568137)

p.150 Mark Freeman – licenced under the Creative Commons Attribution
2.0 Generic Licence (www.flickr.com/photos/46357488@N00/398878345)

p.151 John Wright – licenced under the Creative Commons Attribution 2.0
Generic Licence (www.flickr.com/photos/dryfish/3622133836)

p.155 Prashant Ram – licenced under the Creative Commons Attribution-
NoDerivs 2.0 Generic Licence (www.flickr.com/photos/stupid_
dream/9595136019)

THE UGLY GAME

56 André Zehetbauer – licenced under the Creative Commons
tribution-Share Alike 2.0 Generic Licence (www.flickr.com/photos/
ı1172/2287052418/in/photolist-nTobFm-nToqEx-gZkvC-4u6K1f-
ɔ35M2V-ojgQ2D-ojwr3U-ojypJv-ojniVY-o3ST8x-oaSTkF-oaNcQJ-
o3GgwH-o4ukqb-7fDu1u-ojgDVB-o34LVB-o34xRG-ok6mKZ-3tbTVS-
ck486j)

p.157 © judylcrook, reproduced by kind permission (www.flickr.com/
photos/jlcrook/)

p.160 Carl De Souza/AFP/Getty Images

p.161 Kumar Appaiah – licenced under the Creative Commons
Attribution-Share Alike 2.0 Generic Licence (www.flickr.com/photos/
akumar/8306967347/)

p.162 Laurence Griffiths/Getty Images

p.163 BBC

p.164 Phil Hawksworth – licenced under the Creative Commons Attribution
2.0 Generic Licence (www.flickr.com/photos/philhawksworth/9515994803/
in/photolist-fuTXHV-4VQYyY)

p.165 Rishad Daroowala – licenced under the Creative Commons
Attribution-NoDerivs 2.0 Generic Licence (www.flickr.com/photos/
rishadd/8092627525/in/photolist-jjwNRg-dk7QdM-rGhRG-dk7NDg-
8ZYb5H-oeF2Au-rGgjE-siKTb-h1yKRt-hn5Xtu-rGgmv-rGggy-rGgcq-
fEe4Rw-rCQ7t-rGgth-rGgiX-rGgvp-rGgy3-rGgqS-auRBTd-7svFBX-
6YHsfd-ep7tLv-8QhGvu-8hkbtV-94n63Q-atiL8i-dPgret-atmpMb-atmpCC-
96YdCw-aB4MZU-atmpFd-atiL5M-atmpNL-atmprw-54p9zv-rGgeD-
rGgoX-7weYye-g2o7xx-2Upa9m-8Nnvsh-7a4Dm8-7YHfxW-dkr7Sh-
9VcF9g-dPn5Zw-8yX3b)

p.166 Akio Takemoto – licenced under the Creative Commons
Attribution-Share Alike 2.0 Generic Licence (www.flickr.com/photos/
akiotakemoto/14924053282)

p.167 greezer.ch – licenced under the Creative Commons
Attribution-NoDerivs 2.0 Generic Licence (www.flickr.com/photos/
greeezer/5601439316)

p.168 D.C.Atty – licenced under the Creative Commons Attribution 2.0
Generic Licence (www.flickr.com/photos/figgenhoffer/3628518782/in/
photolist-6wD7dE-6XG1xa-75fdpB-8vV2iZ-6XarFB-6WQ44z-6ftt5a-
55VrTq-55xvwN-6A2p9R-4FTTrh-4VNLGv)

p.169 Mark Freeman – licenced under the Creative Commons Attribution
2.0 Generic Licence (www.flickr.com/photos/46357488@N00/398878345)